THE NEW
CHILDREN'S ILLUSTRATED
ATLAS OF
THE WORLD

Keith Lye

COURAGE
BOOKS

AN IMPRINT OF RUNNING PRESS
PHILADELPHIA · LONDON

Copyright ©1999 by Digital Wisdom Publishing Ltd.
All rights reserved under the Pan-American and International Copyright Conventions
Printed in Hong Kong.

9   8   7   6   5   4   3   2
Digit on the right indicates the number of this printing

Library of Congress Cataloging-in-Publication Number 99-75105

ISBN 0-7624-0643-7

Editor: Marc Phillips
Designers: Nigel Soper, Alex Charles
Cartography: Nicholas Rowland
Maps: Copyright © Digital Wisdom Publishing Ltd.

This book may be ordered by mail from the publisher.
Please include $2.50 for postage and handling.
But try your bookstore first!

Published by Courage Books, an imprint of
Running Press Book Publishers
125 South Twenty-second Street
Philadelphia, Pennsylvania 19103-4399

Visit us on the web!
www.runningpress.com

EUROPE Pages 20-31

AFRICA Pages 44-49

Contents

Keys to maps and symbols

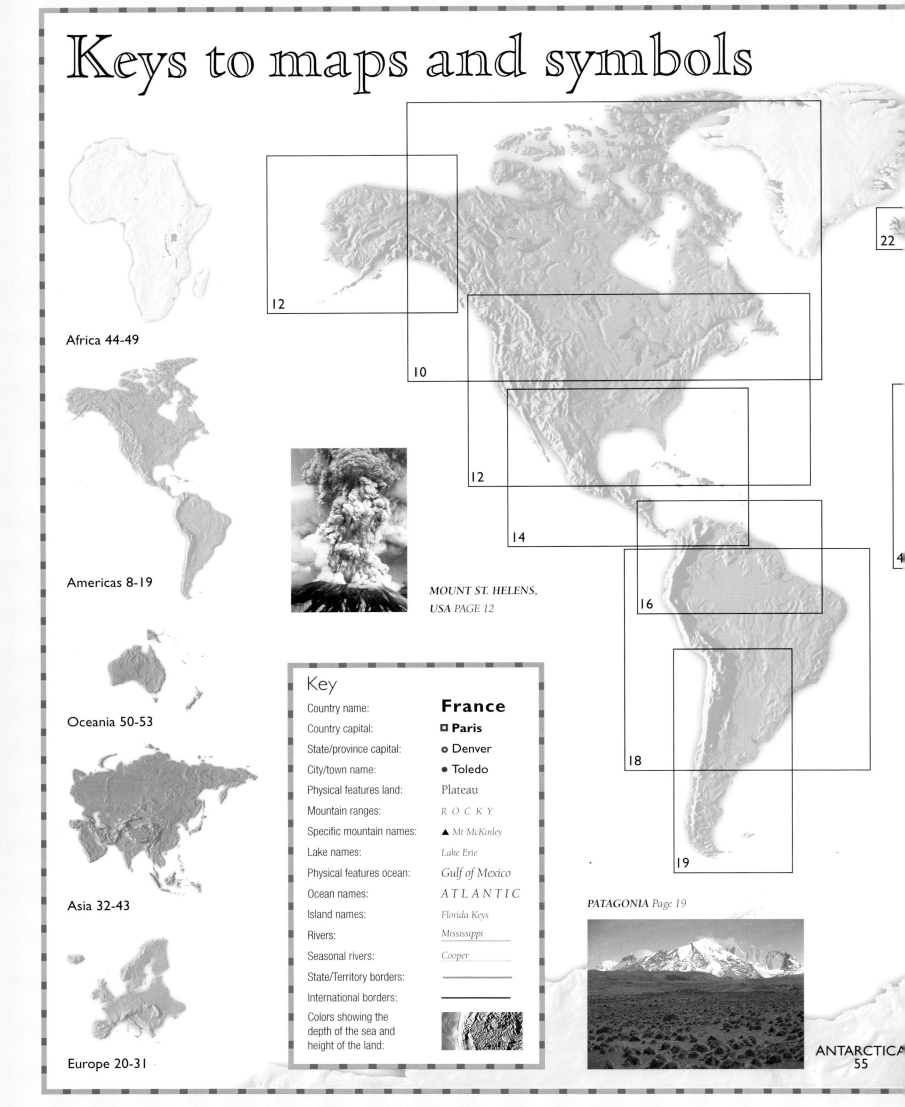

Africa 44-49

Americas 8-19

Oceania 50-53

Asia 32-43

Europe 20-31

12

10

12

14

16

18

19

22

MOUNT ST. HELENS, USA PAGE 12

Key

Country name:	**France**
Country capital:	▫ **Paris**
State/province capital:	◦ Denver
City/town name:	● Toledo
Physical features land:	Plateau
Mountain ranges:	*R O C K Y*
Specific mountain names:	▲ *Mt McKinley*
Lake names:	*Lake Erie*
Physical features ocean:	*Gulf of Mexico*
Ocean names:	*A T L A N T I C*
Island names:	*Florida Keys*
Rivers:	*Mississippi*
Seasonal rivers:	*Cooper*
State/Territory borders:	———
International borders:	———
Colors showing the depth of the sea and height of the land:	

PATAGONIA Page 19

ANTARCTICA
55

Arctic Ocean
54

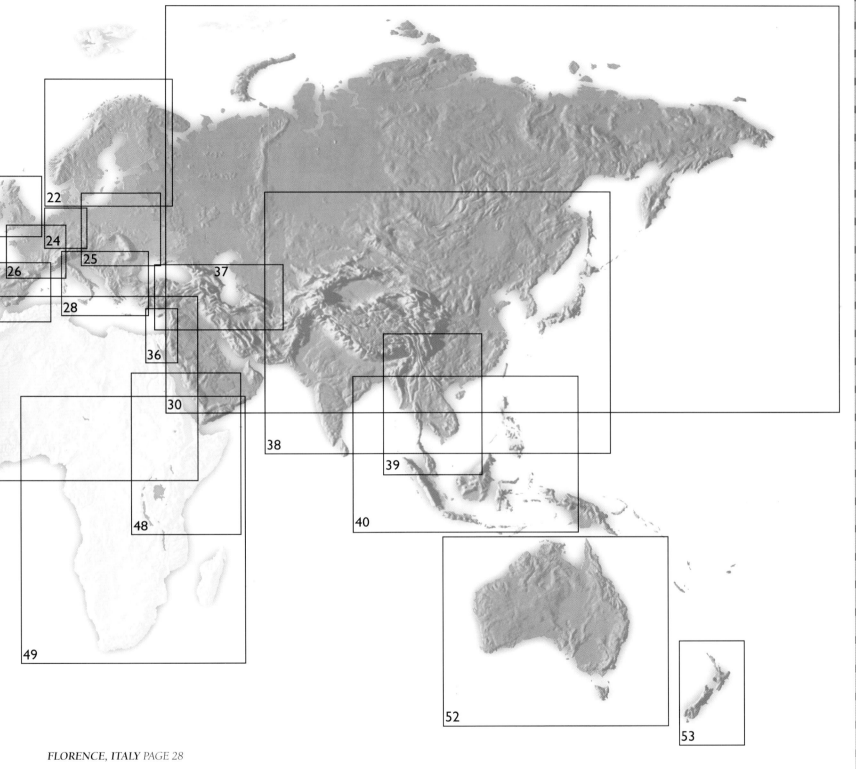

22

24

25

37

26

28

36

30

38

39

40

48

49

52

53

FLORENCE, ITALY PAGE 28

SOUTHEAST ASIA PAGE 41

SINGAPORE PAGE 40

TEMPERATE FORESTS

Deciduous forests, consisting of trees that shed their leaves in the fall, once covered large areas in the world's temperate regions. Much of this forest has been cut down to create farmland.

TROPICAL SAVANNA

Tropical savanna (grassland with scattered trees) occurs in places with hot climates. Savanna regions have a long dry season. In Africa, the tropical savanna is the home of elephants, lions, giraffes and many other animals.

DESERTS

Deserts cover about a fifth of the world's land area. Sand dunes cover some deserts. Other deserts are gravel-strewn or salt-covered plains. Areas of bare rock are also common to deserts.

TROPICAL FORESTS

Tropical forests occur where rain falls throughout the year, though monsoon forests grow in places where most of the rain is confined to one season. Tropical forests are being rapidly destroyed by loggers, or simply cleared for mining, hydroelectric schemes and ranching.

The World

The Earth is the fifth largest planet in the Solar System. It is a rocky body, but water covers about 71 percent of its surface. Most of the land is divided into seven continents. In order of size, they are Asia, Africa, North America, South America, Antarctica, Europe, and Australia.

By area, the world's largest countries are Russia, Canada, China, the United States, and Brazil. But the countries with the largest populations are China, India, the United States, Indonesia, and Brazil.

1. Gibraltar (U.K)	15. Hungary		
2. Andorra	16. Croatia		
3. Monaco	17. Bosnia-Herzegovina		
4. Vatican City	18. Yugoslavia		
5. San Marino	19. Albania		
6. Liechtenstein	20. Macedonia		
7. Switzerland	21. Modova		
8. Luxembourg	22. Kalingrad (Russia)		
9. Belgium	23. Armenia		
10. Netherlands	24. Azerbajan		
11. Czech Republic	25. Kuwait		
12. Austria	26. Bahrain		
13. Slovak Republic	27. Qatar		
14. Slovenia	28. United Arab Emirates		

Afghanistan	35	Bangladesh	38	Burkina Faso	46
Albania	29	Barbados	15	Burundi	48
Algeria	46	Belarus	30	Cambodia	39
Andorra	27	Belgium	24	Cameroon	47
Angola	49	Belize	15	Canada	10
Antigua and Barbuda	15	Benin	46	Cape Verde	46
Argentina	19	Bhutan	38	Central African Republic	49
Armenia	37	Bolivia	18	Chad	47
Australia	52	Bosnia & Herzegovina	29	Chile	19
Austria	24	Botswana	49	China	42
Azerbaijan	30	Brazil	18	Colombia	16
Bahamas	15	Brunei	41	Comoros	45
Bahrain	35	Bulgaria	29	Congo, Democratic Republic of	49

POLAR REGIONS

Polar climates include regions where ice and snow cover the land throughout the year. In tundra regions, the snow melts in summer. Plants grow quickly, attracting many animals and birds.

CONIFEROUS FORESTS

Evergreen coniferous forests cover vast areas in northern Canada, northern Europe, and northern Russia. Coniferous trees, such as fir and pine, are well adapted to survive the long, snowy winters.

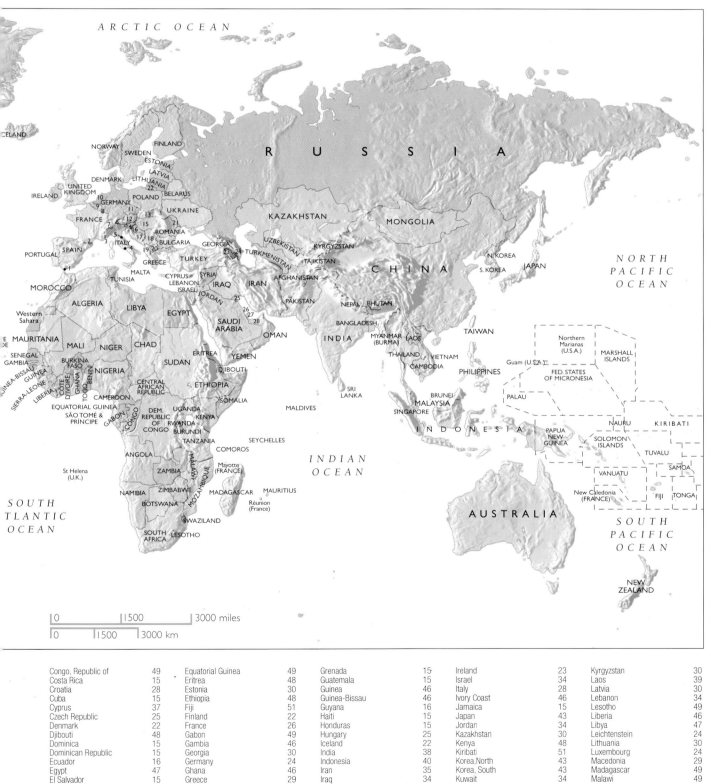

0 1500 3000 miles
0 1500 3000 km

The Americas

FROZEN The Americas are a land of extremes, from the cold snowy north, the hot dry deserts of the southwest, and subtropical swamps of the southeast.

ARCTIC OCEAN

Greenland (DENMARK)

ICELAND

BEAUFORT SEA

Baffin Bay

Alaska (U.S.A.)

Davis Strait

Hudson Bay

C A N A D A

Ottawa □

UNITED STATES OF AMERICA

Washington D.C. □

Bermuda (U.K.)

Gulf of Mexico

BAHAMAS □Nassau

Havana □ CUBA

DOMINICAN REPUBLIC

MEXICO

HAITI

Puerto Rico (U.S.A.)

JAMAICA

Mexico City □

BELIZE HONDURAS

CARIBBEAN SEA

TRINIDAD & TOBAGO

GUATEMALA

EL SALVADOR

NICARAGUA

COSTA RICA PANAMA

North America and South America were once called the New World. This is because they were unknown in Europe until the voyages of Christopher Columbus in the late 15th century.

North America includes Greenland, Canada, the United States, Mexico, the seven countries of Central America, and the island countries in the Caribbean. Northern North America is cold with long, snowy winters and short summers. To the south, the climate becomes warmer. The equator runs through northern South America. Both northern and central South America are hot and rainy. This region contains the world's largest rainforest. In the far south is the cold and windswept Cape Horn, Chile.

The ancestors of the Native Americans reached North America from Asia around 15,000 years ago. They gradually moved south reaching every part of the Americas. They founded great civilizations in Mexico, Central America and the Andes Mountains. In the 16th century, Europeans began to explore and colonize the Americas. Today, the Americas have a mixed population, with immigrants from all over the world. Canada and the United States are among the world's richest countries. But many Latin American countries are poor.

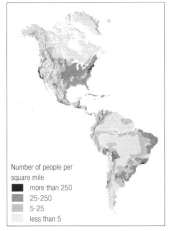

Number of people per square mile
- more than 250
- 25-250
- 5-25
- less than 5

POPULATION

North America has 462 million people, as compared with 330 million in South America. The United States of America and Brazil are the countries that have the largest populations.

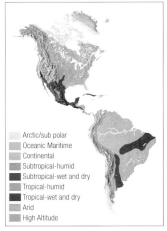

- Arctic/sub polar
- Oceanic Maritime
- Continental
- Subtropical-humid
- Subtropical-wet and dry
- Tropical-humid
- Tropical-wet and dry
- Arid
- High Altitude

CLIMATE

The Americas have a full range of climates, ranging from polar in the north, through temperate to tropical. The mountains have different zones of climate depending on the altitude.

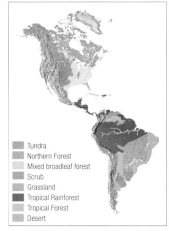

- Tundra
- Northern Forest
- Mixed broadleaf forest
- Scrub
- Grassland
- Tropical Rainforest
- Tropical Forest
- Desert

VEGETATION

Every kind of vegetation zone occurs in the Americas, including ice and treeless tundra in the north, temperate forests, grasslands, desert, and tropical rainforests.

FACT FILE

● English is the chief language in Anglo-America (Canada and the United States). Latin America consists of Mexico, Central America, much of the Caribbean, and South America. There, the chief languages are Spanish, Portuguese (in Brazil), and French.

● Greenland, a province of Denmark, is the world's largest island.

● The world's largest rainforest grows in the Amazon River basin. It covers roughly two-fifths of South America.

SAN FRANCISCO
The Golden Gate Bridge extends across the entrance to San Francisco Bay.

CARACAS, VENEZUELA
Caracas, capital of Venezuela, is a busy modern city, where traffic jams are common.

```
0          500          1000 miles
0       500      1000 km
```

CARIBBEAN SEA

Caracas
VENEZUELA
GUYANA
SURINAM
French Guiana

Bogota
COLOMBIA

Quito
ECUADOR

BRAZIL

PERU
Lima

La Paz
BOLIVIA
Brasilia

PACIFIC OCEAN

CHILE
PARAGUAY
Asunción

ATLANTIC OCEAN

URUGUAY
Santiago
Buenos Aires
Montevideo

ARGENTINA

Falkland Is.
(U.K.)

TV IN THE FOREST
In forest villages in Brazil, television is an important means of communication.

RIO DE JANEIRO
Soccer is popular throughout Latin America, including the beaches at the Brazilian city of Rio de Janeiro.

Canada

Canada is the world's second largest country after Russia. The north contains ice caps, a treeless tundra zone, and vast forests, containing such trees as fir, pine and spruce. Most Canadians live in the south. Canada has a population of approximately 30,287,000, including 30,000 Inuit and about 440,000 Native Americans. However, most people are of British or French origin.

Farming, ranching, forestry, and fishing are important activities. Canada produces oil and natural gas, together with copper, gold, iron, uranium, and zinc. The country manufactures cars, chemicals, electronic goods, food products, machinery, and timber products.

INUIT

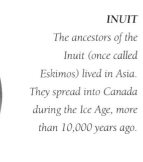

The ancestors of the Inuit (once called Eskimos) lived in Asia. They spread into Canada during the Ice Age, more than 10,000 years ago.

VANCOUVER

Vancouver, British Columbia, is Canada's third largest city.

FACT FILE

● Canada is a federation of ten provinces and three territories. The largest provinces are Quebec and Ontario.

● A new territory for the Inuit was created in 1999. Called Nunavut, it was formerly part of Northwest Territories.

● Canada is the world's leading producer of cobalt ore, uranium and zinc ore.

● Farmland covers only eight percent of Canada. The rest of the land is either too cold or too rugged for farming.

● More than 7 million Canadians are of French origin. Most French-speaking people live in the province of Quebec.

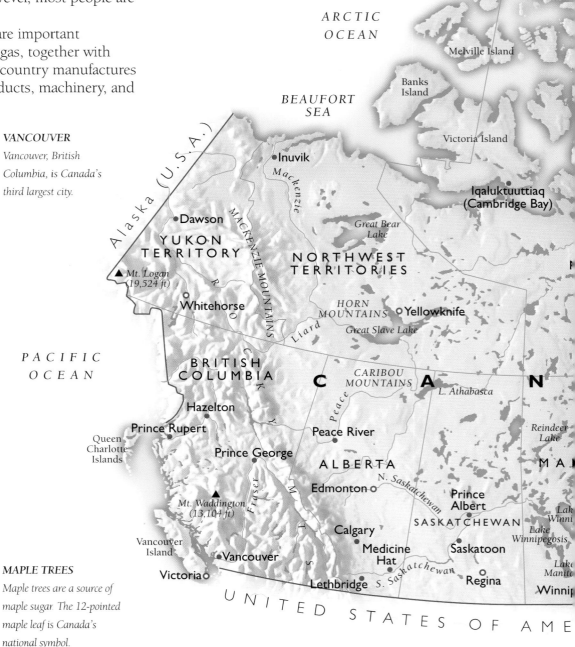

MAPLE TREES

Maple trees are a source of maple sugar. The 12-pointed maple leaf is Canada's national symbol.

CANADA GEESE

The Canada goose, North America's common wild goose, breeds in northern Canada and flies south in summer.

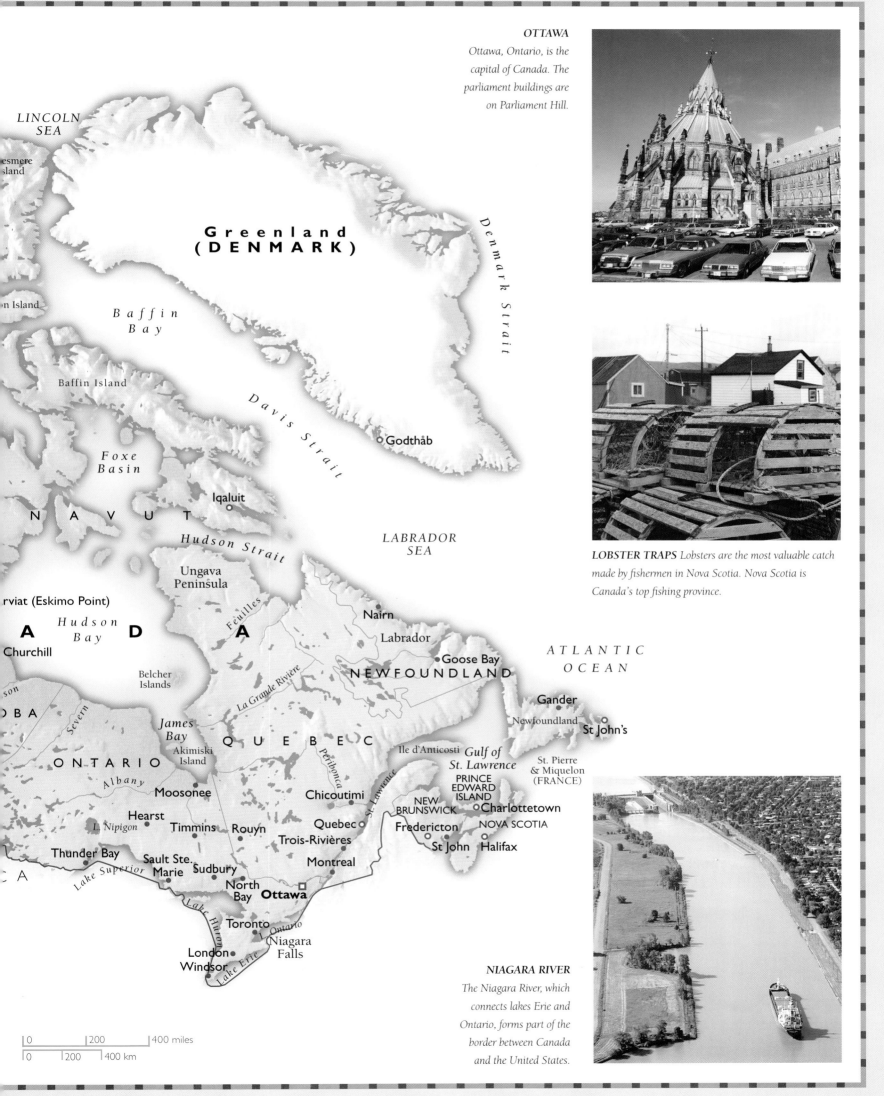

LINCOLN
SEA

esmere
sland

n Island

**Greenland
(DENMARK)**

Baffin
Bay

Baffin Island

Denmark Strait

Davis Strait

Foxe
Basin

○ Godthåb

Iqaluit ○

N A V U T

Hudson Strait

LABRADOR
SEA

Ungava
Peninsula

rviat (Eskimo Point)

Hudson
Bay

Feuilles

Churchill

A   A

Nairn

Labrador

Belcher
Islands

● Goose Bay

La Grande Rivière

N E W F O U N D L A N D

ATLANTIC
OCEAN

son

OBA

Severn

James
Bay

Akimiski
Island

Gander ●

Newfoundland

St John's ●

ONTARIO

Albany

Moosonee ●

Péribonca

Ile d'Anticosti

*Gulf of
St. Lawrence*

St. Pierre
& Miquelon
(FRANCE)

Chicoutimi ●

Q U E B E C

PRINCE
EDWARD
ISLAND

● Charlottetown

Hearst ●

L. Nipigon

Timmins ●

Rouyn ●

Quebec ●

St. Lawrence

NEW
BRUNSWICK

NOVA SCOTIA

Thunder Bay ●

Trois-Rivières ●

Fredericton ●

Sault Ste.
Marie ●

Sudbury ●

Montreal ●

St John ●

Halifax ●

Lake Superior

North
Bay ●

□ **Ottawa**

C A

Lake Huron

Toronto ●

Ontario

Niagara
Falls

London ●

Windsor ●

Lake Erie

| 0 | 200 | 400 miles |
| 0 | 200 | 400 km |

OTTAWA
*Ottawa, Ontario, is the
capital of Canada. The
parliament buildings are
on Parliament Hill.*

LOBSTER TRAPS *Lobsters are the most valuable catch
made by fishermen in Nova Scotia. Nova Scotia is
Canada's top fishing province.*

NIAGARA RIVER

*The Niagara River, which
connects lakes Erie and
Ontario, forms part of the
border between Canada
and the United States.*

United States of America

The United States is the world's fourth largest country. It has varied scenery, with broad coastal plains in the east, together with the Great Plains drained by the Mississippi River between the Appalachian and Rocky Mountains. It has huge forests, subtropical beaches in Hawaii and Florida, grasslands called prairies, and deserts.

The country is the world's richest and most developed. Its resources include oil, natural gas, coal and a wide range of metals. Farming is highly mechanized and the country leads the world in its total farm production. Manufacturing is the most valuable economic activity. Manufactured products include chemicals, food products, machinery, metal goods, printed goods, and vehicles.

MOUNT ST. HELENS
Mount St. Helens, Washington state, erupted in 1980.

LOS ANGELES *Los Angeles, California, is the second largest city in the United States. It has a population of about 3,550,000.*

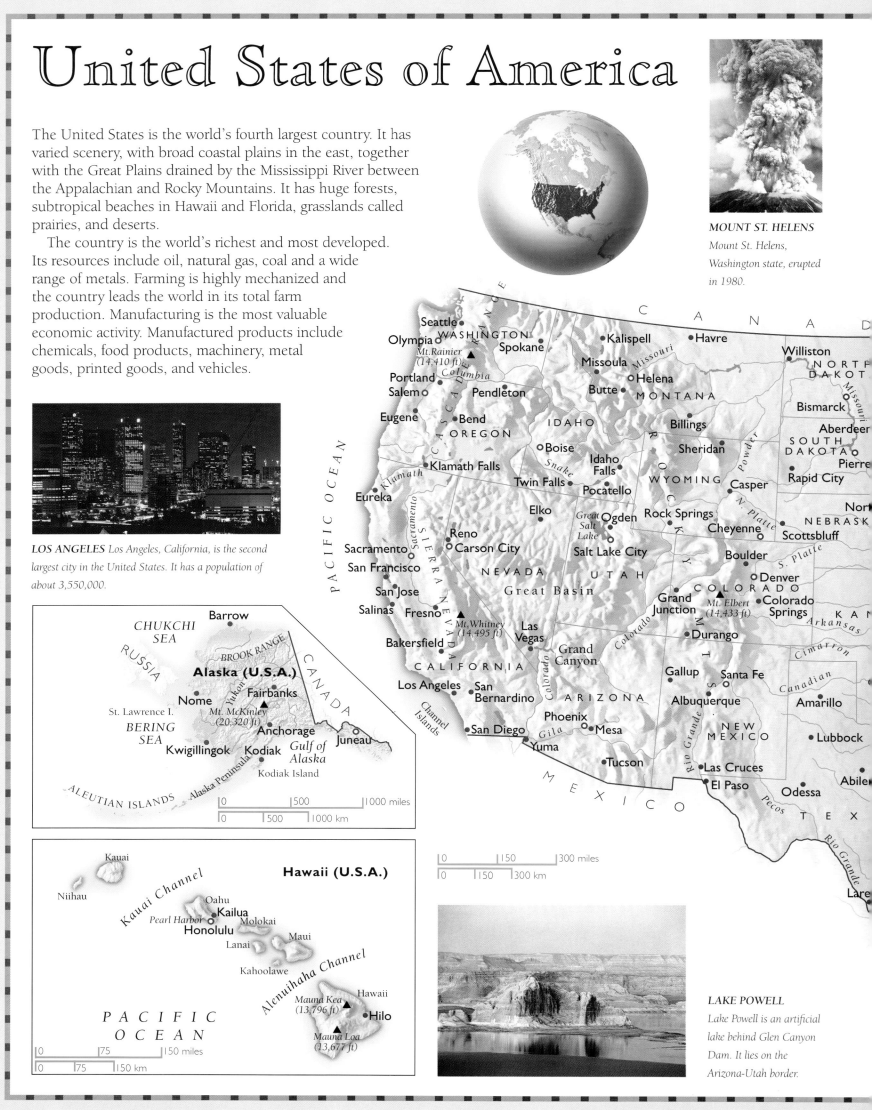

LAKE POWELL
Lake Powell is an artificial lake behind Glen Canyon Dam. It lies on the Arizona-Utah border.

MOUNT RUSHMORE *Carved heads of U.S. presidents can be seen at Mount Rushmore, South Dakota.*

LAS VEGAS *Built shortly after World War II in the Nevada desert, Las Vegas is famous for its gambling casinos.*

NEW YORK CITY *New York City is the largest city in the United States. The Brooklyn Bridge connects Brooklyn to Manhattan.*

MAINE
Augusta
VERMONT
Montpelier
NEW HAMPSHIRE
Concord
MASSACHUSETTS
Boston
Cape Cod
Providence
RHODE ISLAND
Hartford
CONNECTICUT
New York City
NEW JERSEY
Trenton
ATLANTIC OCEAN

Grand Forks
MINNESOTA
Duluth
Lake Superior
Marquette
Lake Huron
WISCONSIN
St Paul Eau Claire
Minneapolis Green Bay MICHIGAN
Milwaukee Grand Rapids Flint
Madison Lansing Detroit
IOWA Lake Michigan
Chicago Gary
Sioux City
Des Moines Cedar Rapids
Peoria INDIANA
ILLINOIS
Jefferson City Springfield Indianapolis Cincinnati
Topeka Kansas City St. Louis Evansville Lexington
Wichita MISSOURI KENTUCKY
Springfield Nashville Knoxville
TENNESSEE
Tulsa ARKANSAS Chattanooga
OKLAHOMA Fort Smith Memphis
Oklahoma City Little Rock MISSISSIPPI
Dallas Shreveport Jackson Birmingham
Fort Worth LOUISIANA ALABAMA
Waco Mobile Montgomery
Baton Rouge Biloxi Pensacola
Austin Houston New Orleans
San Antonio Galveston Mississippi Delta
Corpus Christi

Lake Ontario
Rochester Albany
Lake Erie Buffalo Scranton
Erie PENNSYLVANIA
Toledo Akron Philadelphia
Cleveland Pittsburgh Harrisburg
OHIO Dover
Columbus WASHINGTON D.C. DELAWARE
Dayton Annapolis
WEST VIRGINIA MARYLAND
Frankfort Charleston Richmond Chesapeake Bay
VIRGINIA Norfolk
Roanoke
Greensboro Raleigh Cape Hatteras
NORTH CAROLINA
Charlotte
Wilmington
SOUTH CAROLINA Cape Fear
Columbia
Augusta Charleston
Atlanta
Macon
Columbus Savannah
GEORGIA
Albany
Jacksonville
Tallahassee Daytona Beach
Orlando Cape Canaveral
Tampa FLORIDA
St. Petersburg L. Okeechobee
Miami
Key West Florida Keys

Mississippi
Missouri
Arkansas
Red River
Brazos
Tennessee
Alabama
APPALACHIAN MTS

Gulf of Mexico

MIAMI *Florida's subtropical climate makes it one of the most popular tourist destinations in the United States.*

ROAD TRANSPORT *The United States has more than 50 cars for every 100 people. This highway junction in San Francisco was built to cope with the heavy traffic.*

WHITE HOUSE *The White House, Washington D.C., is the official home of the president.*

FACT FILE

● The United States contains 50 states plus Washington D.C. (District of Columbia). Alaska and Hawaii became the 49th and 50th states in 1959.

● The Grand Canyon, Arizona, is up to 1 mile (1.6 km) deep in places.

● Mauna Kea, Hawaii, is the world's highest mountain, measured from the sea floor. Its total height is 33,481 ft (10,205 m), but only 13,796 ft (4,205 m) appears above sea level.

● The world's biggest bear, the Kodiak bear, is found in Alaska.

● The US flag, the 'Stars and Stripes', has 13 stripes to represent the 13 original colonies, with 50 stars to symbolize the states.

Mexico, Central America and the Caribbean

GUATEMALA *Goods are often carried in baskets on the head.*

Mexico and the seven Central American countries, together with the islands in the Caribbean, lie mainly in the tropics. The Caribbean islands are divided into two main groups. The Greater Antilles includes the larger islands, such as Cuba. The Lesser Antilles is made up of small islands.

Hot deserts are found in northern Mexico, but most Mexicans live on the high central plateau, which is dotted with active volcanoes. Central America also has many volcanoes, with steamy rainforests growing on their slopes. Mexico has large oil deposits and industries, but farming and tourism are the leading activities in much of Central America and the Caribbean.

FACT FILE

● The world's second longest coral reef, after Australia's Great Barrier Reef, lies off the coast of Belize. It has no name.
● When Mount Pelee exploded on the island of Martinique in 1902, a cloud of hot gas and ash killed all but two people in the nearby town of St Pierre.
● Costa Rica has no army. The army was abolished in 1948 following a civil war.
● Hurricanes often strike the Caribbean and Central America. In 1998, in Central America, more than 7,000 people died in floods and mudslides caused by a violent hurricane.
● Mexico City is one of the world's largest cities. It has a population of more than 16 million. Many people live in slums around the city.

RAIN FORESTS
The rain forests are under great threat from loggers.

PANAMA CANAL
The 50.7-mile (81.6-km) Panama Canal links the Atlantic and Pacific oceans and provides a short cut for ships.

MAYA The great Mayan empire, founded between 250AD and 900AD in Central America, is recalled today by actors.

TROPICAL FRUITS Mangos, pineapples and citrus fruits are major products in the region. The primary fruit export, however, is bananas.

TOBACCO Cuba has a large tobacco industry. Its Havana cigars, named after the capital city, are world-famous, .

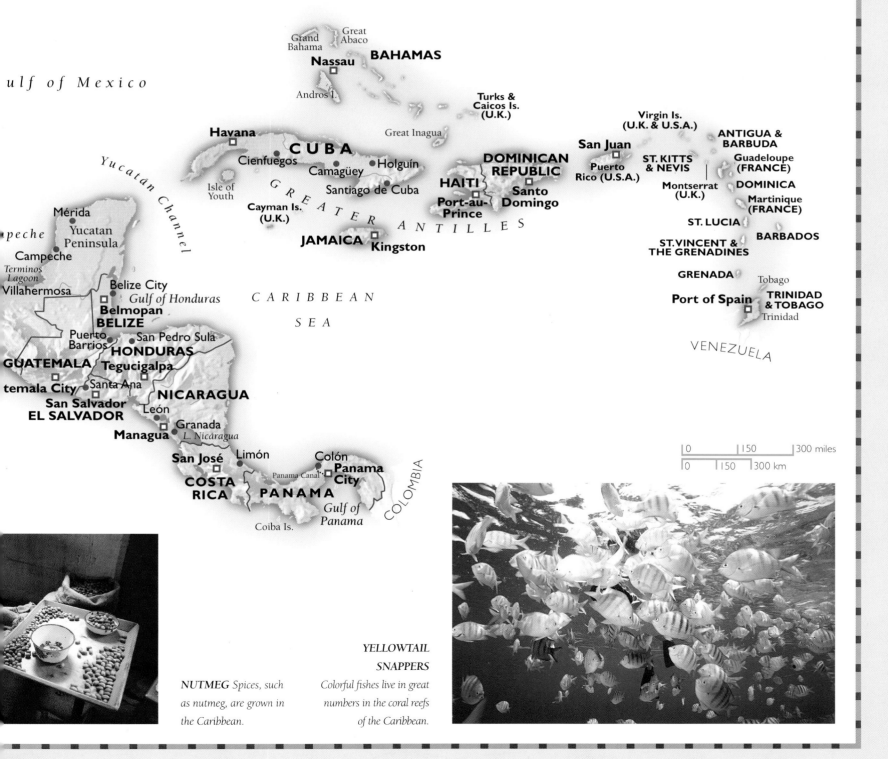

Gulf of Mexico

Grand Bahama
Great Abaco
BAHAMAS
Nassau
Andros I.
Turks & Caicos Is. (U.K.)
Great Inagua
Virgin Is. (U.K. & U.S.A.)
San Juan
ANTIGUA & BARBUDA
Havana
CUBA
Cienfuegos
Camagüey
Holguín
DOMINICAN REPUBLIC
Puerto Rico (U.S.A.)
ST. KITTS & NEVIS
Guadeloupe (FRANCE)
Yucatán Channel
Isle of Youth
Santiago de Cuba
HAITI
Santo Domingo
Montserrat (U.K.)
DOMINICA
Cayman Is. (U.K.)
Port-au-Prince
Martinique (FRANCE)
Mérida
Yucatan Peninsula
peche
Campeche
Terminos Lagoon
Villahermosa
G R E A T E R   A N T I L L E S
JAMAICA
Kingston
ST. LUCIA
ST. VINCENT & THE GRENADINES
BARBADOS
Belize City
Gulf of Honduras
Belmopan
BELIZE
GRENADA
Tobago
Port of Spain
TRINIDAD & TOBAGO
Trinidad
Puerto Barrios
San Pedro Sula
HONDURAS
GUATEMALA
Tegucigalpa
C A R I B B E A N
S E A
VENEZUELA
temala City
Santa Ana
NICARAGUA
San Salvador
EL SALVADOR
León
Managua
Granada
L. Nicaragua
San José
Limón
Colón
Panama City
COSTA RICA
Panama Canal
PANAMA
Gulf of Panama
Coiba Is.
COLOMBIA

0	150	300 miles
0	150	300 km

YELLOWTAIL SNAPPERS
Colorful fishes live in great numbers in the coral reefs of the Caribbean.

NUTMEG Spices, such as nutmeg, are grown in the Caribbean.

Northern South America

Northern South America includes five countries and one territory, French Guiana, an overseas Department of France.

In the west lies the northern part of the Andes Mountains, the world's longest range. It contains volcanoes which erupt from time to time. Earthquakes are also common in this region. East of the Andes lie broad plains drained by tributaries of the Orinoco and Amazon rivers. Tropical grassland, called llanos, covers parts of Venezuela. But rainforest, called selva, covers most of the land, including the Guiana Highlands in the east.

Oil-rich Venezuela is the richest country, while Guyana is the poorest country in South America. Farming and forestry are leading activities in northern South America.

QUITO *Quito, the capital of Ecuador, lies just south of the equator.*

FACT FILE

● Kourou, French Guiana, is the European Space Agency's rocket launching station.
● Angel Falls, in eastern Venezuela, is the world's highest waterfall. It has a total height of 3,212 ft (979 m).
● Guyana used to be called British Guiana and Surinam was once called Dutch Guiana.
● South America's only bear is the spectacled bear found in the high Andes.
● Ecuador is Spanish for 'equator'. The equator runs through Ecuador, near the capital Quito.
● The Galapagos Islands, which belong to Ecuador, lie about 600 miles (970 km) west of Ecuador in the Pacific Ocean.
● Devil's Island, an island off the coast of French Guiana, was the site of a brutal prison camp. It was closed in 1945.

BLOWPIPES

Arrows with poisonous tips are still used by Ecuador's native American Indians to kill animals.

ORINOCO RIVER

The Orinoco is Venezuela's chief river

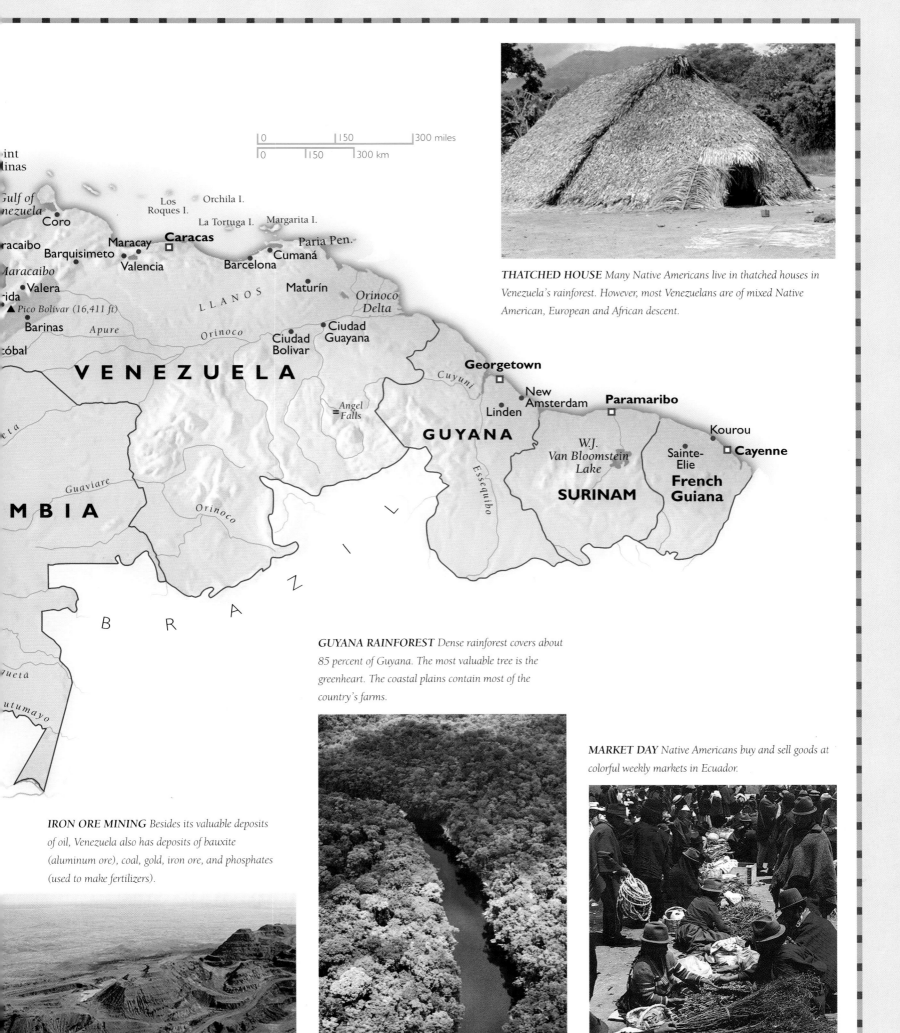

0 | 150 | 300 miles
0 | 150 | 300 km

THATCHED HOUSE *Many Native Americans live in thatched houses in Venezuela's rainforest. However, most Venezuelans are of mixed Native American, European and African descent.*

GUYANA RAINFOREST *Dense rainforest covers about 85 percent of Guyana. The most valuable tree is the greenheart. The coastal plains contain most of the country's farms.*

MARKET DAY *Native Americans buy and sell goods at colorful weekly markets in Ecuador.*

IRON ORE MINING *Besides its valuable deposits of oil, Venezuela also has deposits of bauxite (aluminum ore), coal, gold, iron ore, and phosphates (used to make fertilizers).*

Central South America

Central South America contains Peru, Bolivia, and Brazil, a country larger than Australia. Brazil contains most of the Amazon basin and its huge rainforest. Other regions include the dry northeast, and the southeast, which contains most of the large cities. Brazil is a fast-developing country, but Bolivia and Peru, despite their rich mineral deposits, are much poorer.

IGUAÇU FALLS *The Iguaçu Falls are a scenic tourist attraction on the Brazil-Argentine border.*

VENEZUELA

GUYANA

SURINAM

French Guyana

GUIANA HIGHLANDS

COLOMBIA

ECUADOR

Pico da Neblina
(9,888 ft)

Branco

Negro

Japurá

Macapá

Marajó Bay

Marajó I.

Amazon

Belèm

São Marcos Bay

São Luis

Fortaleza

Teresina

Mossoró

Natal

Recife

SERTÃO

Manaus

Santarém

Tocantins

Putumayo

Iquitos

Marañón

S E L V A S

Madeira

Tapajos

Xingu

Araguaia

Parnaiba

São Francisco

Piura

Chiclayo

Juruá

Purus

Pôrto Velho

Aripuana

Sobradinho Reservoir

Maceió

Trujillo

Pucallpa

Ucayali

Rio Branco

Jiparaná

B R A Z I L

Aracaju

Chimbote

Huascarán
(22,205 ft)

SERRA DOS PARECIS

Arinos

Salvador

P E R U

Mamoré

Guaporé

MATO GROSSO PLATEAU

Ilhéus

Callao

Lima

Huancayo

Machu Picchu

Cuzco

Ica

El Misti
(19,101 ft)

Ancohume
(21,490 ft)

Cuiabá

□**Brasília**

BRAZILIAN HIGHLANDS

Nazca

L. Titicaca

BOLIVIA

Goiânia

Doce

Arequipa

□La Paz

Cochabamba

Santa Cruz

Campo Grande

Uberlândia

Uberaba

Belo Horizonte

Vitória

ALTIPLANO

Oruro

L. Poopó

Sucre

Ribeirão Prêto

Campinas

Rio de Janeiro

Campos

CHILE

Potosi

Pilcomayo

Parana

São Paulo

Santos

PARAGUAY

Itaipu Res.

Curitiba

ARGENTINA

Iguaçu Falls

SERRA DO MAR

Florianópolis

URUGUAY

Uruguay

Santa Maria

Pôrto Alegre

Patos Lagoon

Mirim Lake

0   300   600 miles
0   300   600 km

FACT FILE

● Brazil is the world's fifth largest country.
● La Paz, Bolivia, the world's highest capital city, is about 11,890 ft (3,624 m) above sea level.
● The Amazon is the world's second longest river, but it carries more water than the Nile, Mississippi, and Chang Jiang (Yangtze) combined.
● The Inca empire in the Andes became important in the 13th century. A Spanish force conquered it between 1532 and 1533.

DEFORESTATION
Loggers are destroying Brazil's forests at a fast rate.

AMAZON BASIN
The rainforest contains an enormous variety of plants and animals.

Southern South America

Argentina is the largest and richest country in southern South America. It contains rich farmland and produces beef, corn (maize), and wool. The country also has oil deposits and many factories in the cities. On the western side of the Andes Mountains, Chile produces copper, wheat, and manufactured goods. Farming is also important in Paraguay and Uruguay.

BUENOS AIRES
Buenos Aires is the capital and chief port of Argentina

MOUNTAIN SCENERY
Chile has a variety of climates and landscapes, and includes the driest place in the world, the Atacama Desert.

PATAGONIA
Patagonia in southern Argentina is a cold, dry plateau east of the Andes Mountains.

COPPER MINE
Copper mines are found in the Atacama Desert and also near Chile's capital, Santiago.

FACT FILE
● More than eight out of ten Argentineans are city dwellers.
● The port of Ushuaia is the world's southernmost town.
● Separating Argentina and Paraguay is the Paraná river which flows over 2,500 miles. The English explorer Sebastian Cabot was the first to sail up it in 1526.

Europe

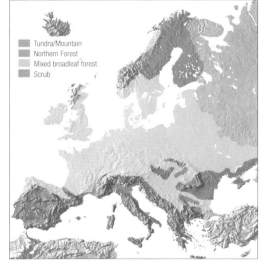

Europe is part of a landmass called Eurasia. In the east, it includes about 25 percent of Russia. Its eastern border runs through the Ural Mountains, the Ural River, the Caspian Sea, and the Caucasus Mountains. Because this border does not follow national boundaries, small parts of Kazakhstan, Azerbaijan and Georgia lie in Europe, as does 3 percent of Turkey. But most people regard these countries as Asian.

Europe is a highly developed continent. Most of its forests have been cleared to make way for farming. Europe also has many industrial cities and living standards are higher than in most of the rest of the world. However, many wars have occurred in Europe and boundaries have changed many times. For example, large-scale changes took place in the early 1990s after the break-up of the former Soviet Union into 15 countries.

FACT FILE

● Europe is the sixth largest continent. Its area, including European Russia, is 4,032,000 sq miles (10,443,000 sq km). This includes about 25 percent of Russia.

● Europe and Asia have a long land boundary. Some people refer to them as a single continent, called Eurasia.

● Ancient Greece and Rome made great contributions to ancient art, government, philosophy and science. Their influence can be seen today all over the world.

● Much of Europe's wildlife is endangered. For example, only about 100 pardel (or Iberian) lynxes survive in the wild.

TOWER BRIDGE

This bridge over the River Thames is one of the landmarks in London.

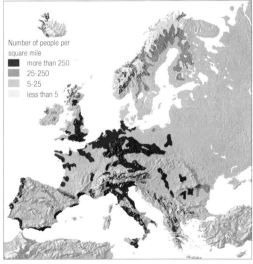

Number of people per square mile
- more than 250
- 25-250
- 5-25
- less than 5

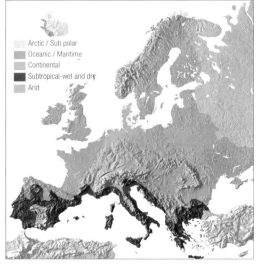

- Arctic / Sub polar
- Oceanic / Maritime
- Continental
- Subtropical-wet and dry
- Arid

- Tundra/Mountain
- Northern Forest
- Mixed broadleaf forest
- Scrub

POPULATION

Excluding Russia, Europe has more than 580 million people. Large areas are thinly populated. But parts of west-central and southern Europe are among the world's most densely populated places.

CLIMATE

A warm ocean current, the Gulf Stream, flows past western Europe giving the area a mild climate. The east has more severe conditions. The climate also changes from the cold north to the warm south.

VEGETATION

Treeless tundra occurs in the far north and the mountains. The northern coniferous forests merge into broadleaf forests in central Europe. Large areas of forest have been cut down and grasslands have been ploughed.

NEUSCHWANSTEIN
This castle in Bavaria, southeastern Germany, was built between 1864 and 1886.

BUDAPEST
Budapest, Hungary, is one of four European capital cities on the River Danube.

BOULES Boules, a form of bowling, is a popular sport in France. But the leading team sport in Europe is soccer.

Reykjavik
ICELAND

COPENHAGEN
Copenhagen is the capital of Denmark.

PISA
Pisa's Leaning Tower is a tourist attraction in Italy.

NORWEGIAN SEA

FINLAND

NORWAY

Helsinki

Oslo □   **SWEDEN**

Stockholm

□ Tallinn
ESTONIA

LATVIA

Scotland

NORTH SEA

BALTIC SEA

LITHUANIA

R U S S I A

ATLANTIC OCEAN

UNITED KINGDOM

IRELAND

Wales   **England**

London □

English Channel

Kaliningrad (RUSSIA)

□ Minsk

□ Kiev

BELARUS

NETHERLANDS

Berlin □

DENMARK
Copenhagen □

POLAND

Warsaw □

BELGIUM

GERMANY

□ Prague
CZECH REP.

Paris □

1

2

Zurich □
SWITZ.

FRANCE

Vienna □
AUSTRIA

SLOVAKIA

Budapest □
HUNGARY

UKRAINE

MOLDOVA

Bay of Biscay

6

5

3

SLOVENIA

CROATIA

BOS.-HERZ.

YUGOSLAVIA

ROMANIA

Bucharest □

BLACK SEA

sbon

Madrid

ITALY

4 — □ Rome

ADRIATIC SEA

BULGARIA
□ Sofia

PORTUGAL

SPAIN

Corsica (FRANCE)

MACEDONIA

ALBANIA

Balearic Is. (SPAIN)

Sardinia (ITALY)

TYRRHENIAN SEA

AEGEAN SEA

Gibraltar (U.K.)

MEDITERRANEAN SEA

IONIAN SEA

GREECE

Athens □

MALTA

Crete (GREECE)

Key to numbered Countries
1. Luxembourg
2. Liechtenstein
3. San Marino
4. Vatican City
5. Monaco
6. Andorra

BARCELONA
Barcelona is Spain's second largest city.

0   200   400 miles

0   200   400 km

Northern Europe

Northern Europe is the coldest and most thinly populated part of Europe. It includes Iceland, Scandinavia (Denmark, Norway and Sweden), and Finland. Iceland depends on fishing, while Norway has valuable oil deposits. Sweden and Denmark are highly developed industrial countries, though Denmark is also known for its dairy and meat products. Forestry is important in Finland.

Northern Norway, Sweden and Finland contain people called Sami (or Lapps). They once followed the migrating herds of reindeer, but many now have permanent homes.

ICELAND

Grimsey · Húsavík · Saudarkrókur · Akureyri · Ólafsvík · Hvítá · Vatnajökull · Keflavík · □ Reykjavik · Heimaey · Vestmannaeyjar

0   100 miles
0   100 km

0   100   200 miles
0   100   200 km

North Cape · Hammerfest · Vadsø · Alta · Tromsø · L. Inari · Lapland · RUSSIA · Vesterålen · Narvik · Kiruna · Sodankylä · Lofoten Is. · Kebnekaise (6,926 ft) · Bodø · Gällivare · Rovaniemi · NORWEGIAN SEA · Boden · Kemi · Mosjøen · Luleå · Piteå · Hailuoto · Oulu · Skellefte · Storuman · Skellefteå · Kajaani · Ume · Umeå · FINLAND · Steinkjer · SWEDEN · Ornsköldsvik · Kuopio · ATLANTIC OCEAN · Trondheim · Ostersund · Vaasa · Joensuu · Gulf of Bothnia · Jyväskylä · Ålesund · Røros · Kramfors · Mikkeli · NORWAY · Sundsvall · Pori · Tampere · Lappeenranta · Hudiksvall · Hämeenlinna · Lahti · Galdhøpiggen (8,100 ft) · Rauma · Lillehammer · Mora · Turku · Vantaa · Kotka · Bergen · Falun · Gävle · Åland · Espoo · □ Helsinki · Gjøvik · Mariehamn · Oslo □ · Haugesund · Drammen · Västerås · Uppsala · Gulf of Finland · Fredrikstad · Karlstad · □ Stockholm · Stavanger · Larvik · Örebro · Södertälje · Egersund · Arendal · Strömstad · Vänern · Norrköping · Kristiansand · Vättern · Linköping · Skagerrak · Gotland · Göteborg · Jönköping · Visby · Ålborg · Kattegat · Halmstad · Växjö · BALTIC SEA · Holstebro · Randers · Kalmar · Öland · DENMARK · Århus · Helsingborg · Karlskrona · Horsens · Kristianstad · Esbjerg · Copenhagen □ · Kolding · Malmö · Rønne · Odense · Bornholm (Denmark) · GERMANY

LITTLE MERMAID
This statue is a famous landmark in Denmark's capital, Copenhagen.

FACT FILE

● The sun does not set in Tromsø, Norway, for three months every year.
● Because of its ice caps and active volcanoes, Iceland is often called the land of ice and fire. Water from hot springs is used to heat homes and offices.
● Finland has about 6,000 lakes.
● Stockholm, capital of Sweden, was built on 14 islands and it has been called the Venice of the North.

STOCKHOLM
The capital of Sweden is a beautiful city and a major port. It was founded in the 13th century.

DOG SLEDDING *Norwegians have developed ways of traveling over snow, such as dog sledding and skiing.*

British Isles

The British Isles contains the Republic of Ireland and the United Kingdom of Great Britain and Northern Ireland. (Great Britain consists of England, Scotland and Wales.) The British Isles also includes the Isle of Man, a British dependency with its own government. The Channel Islands are other British dependencies, but they, too, are self-governing.

The Republic of Ireland was once part of the United Kingdom. It now has important farming, fishing, and manufacturing industries. The United Kingdom is a major industrial and trading nation. Its farms are highly efficient, but the country imports food and raw materials for its industries.

FACT FILE

● Ireland's Irish (Gaelic) name is Eire.
● The British Empire was the largest empire in history. More than 50 former members of the British Empire belong to the Commonwealth of Nations.
● Until 5500 BC, the United Kingdom was joined to mainland Europe.
● The Industrial Revolution began in Britain in the late 17th century.

SHETLAND ISLANDS

Foula   ● Lerwick

Fair Isle

ORKNEY ISLANDS

Cape Wrath

● Kirkwall

● John o'Groats

Thurso

Stornoway

OUTER HEBRIDES   Lewis

St. Kilda

North Uist

South Uist

Barra

Skye

Rhum

Coll

Tiree

Mull

Islay

ATLANTIC OCEAN

North Minch

North West Highlands

Inverness

Loch Ness

Moray Firth

Fraserburgh

Peterhead

Spey

Don

Dee

Aberdeen

Montrose

Ben Nevis (4,406 ft) ▲

GRAMPIAN MTS.

Mallaig

Oban

SCOTLAND

Dundee

Tay

Perth

Glasgow

Edinburgh

Firth of Forth

Holy I.

Clyde

Arran

Ayr

Nith

Tweed

CHEVIOT HILLS

Newcastle upon Tyne

NORTH SEA

Dumfries

Tyne

Durham

Carlisle

Lake District

Middlesbrough

Flamborough Head

Malin Head

Tory I.

Aran I.

Rathlin I.

Stranraer

Isle of Man

Douglas

Blackpool

Preston

Leeds

Bradford

Kingston upon Hull

North Channel

NORTHERN IRELAND

Londonderry

Donegal

Donegal Bay

Lough Neagh

Belfast

Armagh

Sligo

IRISH SEA

Liverpool

Manchester

Sheffield

IRELAND

Dundalk

Achill I.

Lough Corrib

Lough Ree

Athlone

Liffey

Galway Bay

Galway

Dublin

Dun Laoghaire

Holyhead

Wrexham

Derby

The Wash

Norwich

ARAN ISLANDS

Shannon

Lough Derg

Carlow

Snowdon (3,560 ft)

Nottingham

Peterborough

Limerick

Tipperary

Wexford

Cardigan Bay

Wolverhampton

Coventry

Cambridge

Aberystwyth

Birmingham

Northampton

Ipswich

Dingle Bay

Killarney

Waterford

WALES

Cardigan

Wye

Severn

E N G L A N D

Colchester

Carrauntoohill (3,415 ft) ▲

Cork

Carmarthen

Gloucester

Oxford

London

Bantry

Swansea

Cardiff

Reading

Thames

Canterbury

Bristol Channel

Bristol

=Stonehenge

North Downs

Dover

Lundy

Ilfracombe

Shaftsbury

Southampton

South Downs

Folkestone

St. Georges Channel

Barnstaple

Exeter

Bournemouth

Brighton

Dartmoor

Portland Bill

Isle of Wight

Penzance

Plymouth

English Channel

ISLES OF SCILLY

Alderney

CHANNEL ISLANDS

Sark

Guernsey

Jersey

IRELAND

About 42 percent of the people of Ireland live in rural areas.

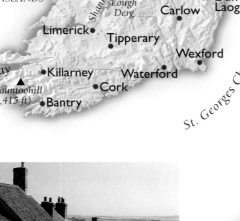

SHAFTESBURY, DORSET

This attractive town, once called Shaston, is featured in many movies and novels.

SCOTLAND *Rural Scotland contains many lakes and beautiful old castles.*

STONEHENGE

This monument in southern England was probably used in ancient times for religious ceremonies.

| 0 | 50 | 100 miles |
| 0 | 50 | 100 km |

West-Central Europe

West-central Europe contains Germany, which lay in ruins after World War II (1939-45). However, Germany recovered quickly and it is now one of the world's top industrial and trading countries. Its many products include cars and other vehicles, computers, electrical equipment, machinery and tools, scientific instruments, ships, steel, and textiles. Germany has many farms but it imports food and many raw materials needed by its industries.

West of Germany are the prosperous Low Countries – Belgium, Netherlands, and Luxembourg. Here, most of the land is flat, but to the south lie mountainous Switzerland, Austria, and tiny Liechtenstein. Switzerland and Austria attract many tourists because of their superb scenery and their winter sports resorts.

BELGIUM

Brussels is the capital and largest city of Belgium.

NETHERLANDS

Clogs are traditional footwear in the Netherlands.

FACT FILE
- Germany ranks second only to the United States in the value of its foreign trade.
- Brussels, capital of Belgium, is also the headquarters of the European Union, a group of 15 nations which work together.
- The Netherlands is often called Holland. But Holland is the name of only part of the country. The people are known as Dutch.
- Belgium has three official languages: Flemish (Dutch) in the north; French in the south; and German in the east.
- Helvetia, the Latin name for Switzerland, appears on Swiss coins and stamps.

GERMANY

Hamburg, in northern Germany, is a major European port.

NETHERLANDS

Tulips and bulbs are among the country's main exports.

SWITZERLAND

The scenic, snowy Alps attract many visitors.

NORTH SEA

DENMARK

BALTIC SEA

Helgoland
Schleswig
Kiel
Cuxhaven
Rostock
Schwerin
West Frisian Islands
Bremerhaven
Emden
Hamburg
Groningen
Bremen
NETHERLANDS
Osnabrück
Hannover
Brandenburg
Berlin
Haarlem
□ **Amsterdam**
Potsdam
The Hague
Utrecht
Brunswick
Magdeburg
Arnhem
Münster
Dessau
Rotterdam
Essen
Dortmund
Münden
Nordhausen
Leipzig
Eindhoven
Düsseldorf
G E R M A N Y
Meissen
Bruges
Antwerp
Cologne
Dresden
Ghent
Maastricht
Marburg
Erfurt
Jena
Chemnitz
Brussels
Liège
Aachen
Bonn
Plauen
BELGIUM
Koblenz
Coburg
Wiesbaden
Frankfurt am Main
Main
Bayreuth
LUXEMBOURG
Trier
Mainz
□ **Luxembourg**
Mannheim
Kitzingen
Nuremberg
Saarbrücken
Heidelberg
Karlsruhe
Ingolstadt
Passau
Linz
Krems
Vienna
Stuttgart
Danube
Steyr
Danube
Bade
Ulm
Augsburg
Neusiedler Lake
Freiburg
Munich
Salzburg
Kapfenberg
Lake Constance
Basel
Zurich
LIECHTENSTEIN
Kitzbühel
A U S T R I A
Neuchâtel
□ **Bern**
Lucerne
□ Vaduz
Innsbruck
▲Grossglockner
Wolfsberg
Graz
L.Neuchâtel
(12,457 ft)
Villach
SWITZERLAND
L.Geneva
Lausanne
St Moritz
Geneva
Martigny
SLOVENIA
Zermatt
Matterhorn
(14,692 ft)

FRANCE
Rhine
Maas
Lek
Ems
Weser
Elbe
Oder
POLAND
Hunsrück
Black Forest
Rhine
Danube
Inn
Main
Bohemian Forest
CZECH REPUBLIC
Enns
Inn
ITALY
HUNG

0 | 50 | 100 miles
0 | 50 | 100 km

Eastern Europe

After World War II, Europe was divided. The Western countries had democratic governments, while the Eastern countries had Communist governments and were allies of the Communist Soviet Union. The Communist East included East Germany, the five countries shown on the map below, and (in southeast Europe) Albania, Bulgaria and the former Yugoslavia. From the late 1980s, Eastern European countries elected democratic governments. Communist policies were ended, but the countries faced problems in developing their changing economies.

Eastern Europe has scenic mountains, broad plains, and attractive ancient cities and towns. Winters are cold, but summers are warm.

POLAND

Power stations and factories burning coal have caused much pollution.

FACT FILE
● The Danube is Europe's second longest river. Four capitals – Belgrade, Bratislava, Budapest, and Vienna – lie on its banks.
● Czestochowa, southern Poland, is the country's chief center for pilgrims.
● The former country of Czechoslovakia spilt into two – the Czech Republic and the Slovak Republic – on January 1, 1993.

BUDAPEST MARKET

Budapest is the capital of Hungary.

PRAGUE

Prague is the capital of the Czech Republic, a country formed in 1993 when the former nation of Czechoslovakia split into two. The other country is called The Slovak Republic.

BALTIC SEA · LITHUANIA · KALININGRAD (RUSSIA) · Gulf of Gdansk · Gdynia · Gdansk · Elblag · Kolobrzeg · Olsztyn · NORTH EUROPEAN PLAIN · Szczecin · Bydgoszcz · Bialystock · Gorzow Wielkopolski · Torun · BELARUS · Plock · Poznan · Warta · Vistula · Bug · Oder · POLAND · Warsaw · Glogow · Kalisz · Lodz · Pilica · Radom · Lublin · Wroclaw · Czestochowa · Kielce · Chelm · Bug · GERMANY · SUDETES MOUNTAINS · Bytom · Vistula · Rzeszow · Karlovy Vary · Pardubice · Krakow · Tarnow · UKRAINE · Prague · Katowice · Bielsko-Biala · Plzen · CZECH REPUBLIC · Ostrava · Olomouc · CARPATHIAN MOUNTAINS · Cesky Budejovice · Zilina · Gerlachovka (8,711 ft) · Presov · Brno · Trencin · Kosice · AUSTRIA · SLOVAK REPUBLIC · Nitra · Miskolc · Mt. Kekes (3,330 ft) · Bratislava · Debrecen · Botosani · MOLDOVA · Gyor · Budapest · Tisza · Satu Mare · Baia Mare · Szombathely · HUNGARY · Oradea · MOLDAVIAN CARPATHIANS · Iasi · L. Balaton · Bekescsaba · Cluj-Napoca · Tîrgu Mures · Siret · Bacau · Kaposvar · Koros · Mures · SLOVENIA · Szeged · Arad · ROMANIA · Pécs · Mures · CROATIA · Timisoara · Deva · Sibiu · Brasov · Galati · Resita · TRANSYLVANIAN ALPS · Moldoveanu (8,343 ft) · Braila · DOBRUJA · YUGOSLAVIA · Jiu · Pitesti · Ploiesti · Olt · Bucharest · Craiova · Slatina · Dunarea (Danube) · Constanta · BULGARIA · Danube

0 75 150 miles
0 75 150 km

France

France is Western Europe's largest country. Mountains rise in the east and south, but there are also scenic hilly areas, especially in the northeast, and lowlands, such as the densely populated Paris basin. Most of France has a mild climate, but the mountains are snowy in winter.

Farmland covers three-fifths of the land and France is famous for such things as its cheeses and wines. Manufacturing is the most valuable activity. Sunny beaches and fascinating old cities make France a leading tourist country. Monaco, a tiny principality (country ruled by a prince) in southeastern France, is also a tourist center.

CHATEAUX
Elegant chateaux (castles) adorn the Loire valley in west-central France.

NOTRE DAME
Notre Dame is a magnificent church on an island in the River Seine, Paris.

ST. TROPEZ
The Riviera in southeast France contains many resorts, including St. Tropez.

FACT FILE

● France is the world's leading producer of quality wines, but it ranks second to Italy in total wine production.

● Nuclear power plants produce more than half of France's electricity supply.

● Monaco is the world's second smallest independent country after Vatican City.

● More than two million tourists visit the beautiful city of Paris every year. Paris is a world center for fashion industries.

FRENCH WINE
Top-quality wines are among France's best known exports.

Iberia

Iberia contains Portugal, Spain, the small country of Andorra in the Pyrenees, and the British territory of Gibraltar in the south. Portugal is one of Europe's poorer countries, but it is developing quickly. Farming and fishing are important, but the manufacturing of things such as machinery, paper products, processed food, and textiles is the most valuable activity.

   Spain contains the Balearic Islands in the Mediterranean Sea, and the Canary Islands in the Atlantic Ocean, west of the African coast. Tourism, agriculture, and manufacturing are all important in Spain. Its manufactured goods include cars, chemicals, electronic goods, processed food, metal goods, steel, and textiles.

PARADORS Beautiful old buildings in Spain have been converted into luxury hotels. Spain is one of the world's top tourist destinations.

CASTLES Spain has many historic buildings, such as the Lacalahorra Castle in Andalusia.

LISBON

Portugal's capital contains many elegant Roman Catholic churches.

FACT FILE

● Iberia is an ancient name for the area now occupied by Spain and Portugal.

● An earthquake destroyed about two-thirds of Portugal's capital, Lisbon, in 1755.

● Spain has changed from a poor agricultural country in the 1950s and 1960s to a modern industrial country today.

● The Arabs conquered Iberia in the AD 710s. They were finally defeated in 1492 when Christian forces conquered Granada.

Italy and the Balkan States

Italy and the Balkan states form two peninsulas (land areas almost surrounded by sea) in southern Europe. Italy has many ancient Roman ruins, which are among its tourist attractions. About 50 years ago, Italy was a mainly agricultural country, but it is now a major industrial power. Italy contains two mini-states: Vatican City, the headquarters of the Roman Catholic Church; and San Marino. Greece, which has many ruins that recall the splendor of ancient Greece, is now one of Europe's poorer countries, though manufacturing is on the rise.

Apart from Greece, the countries in the Balkan peninsula had non-democratic Communist governments from after World War II until the early 1990s. After Communist control ended in Yugoslavia, four of its republics – Slovenia, Croatia, Macedonia, and Bosnia-Herzegovina – became separate countries, while Serbia and Montenegro formed the new Yugoslavia. The break-up of the former Yugoslavia led to much fighting and bloodshed.

FACT FILE

● Vatican City is the world's smallest independent country. It covers only 0.17 sq miles (0.44 sq km) in northwest Rome.
● The first recorded Olympic Games took place in Greece in 1776 BC.
● Mount Etna, Sicily, is a quiet volcano. Like the volcanoes of Hawaii, when it erupts it emits long streams of runny lava.
● In the early 1990s, the former Yugoslavia split up into five separate countries.

BULGARIA
Religion was discouraged under Communism, but many people are now members of the Bulgarian Orthodox Church.

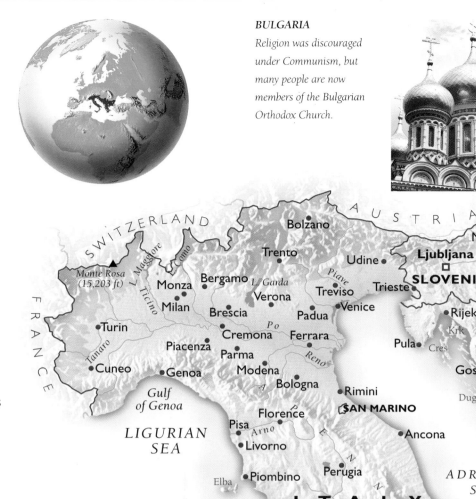

FERRARI
Italy designs and manufactures many of the world's most exotic and beautiful cars.

PARTHENON

The Parthenon is an ancient Greek temple on a hill in Athens, the capital of modern Greece.

GONDOLAS *The beautiful Italian city of Venice is built on and around 120 islands. Boats called gondolas once transported people around the city. But today powerboats have replaced many gondolas.*

OLIVES *Italy and Greece are the world's leading producers of olives.*

H U N G A R Y

Subotica

va Osijek

VOJVODINA

Novi Sad

Belgrade

Bosna Tuzla

nja

ka **SNIA - EGOVINA**

Srebrenica

Sarajevo *Drina*

Mostar

Novi Pazar

MONTENEGRO

brovnik Podgorica

ljet *L. Scutari*

Shkodër

Tiranë

Durrës *L. Ohrid*

Elbasan *L. Prespa*

ALBANIA

Bari Vlore

Taranto

ulf of ranto Gallipoli

YUGOSLAVIA

Kragujevac

SERBIA *Morava*

Krusevac Nis

Leskovac

Pristina

KOSOVO

Skopje

Tetovo *Vardar*

MACEDONIA

Bitola

R O M A N I A

Iskur Vratsa

Sofia *BALKAN MTS*

Pernik

Musala Peak

(9,596 ft) ▲

Pleven

Lovech

Tundzha

Ruse Dobrich

Shumen

Turgovishte Varna

Sliven

Yambol Burgas

BULGARIA

Maritsa

Plovdiv Khaskovo

Smolyan

Struma *RHODOPE MTS*

Drama

Kavála

T U R K E Y

Thásos Samothrace

Thessaloníki Samothrace

Aliakmon Mt Olympus (9,570 ft) ▲

Mt Athos (6,670 ft) ▲

Límnos

Lesbos

Mitílíni

G R E E C E

Kérkira Trikkala Larisa

Corfu *Akheloos*

Párga

Vólos

Skíros

AEGEAN SEA

Chios

Sámos

IONIAN SEA

Leukas

Cephalonia Ithaca

Khalkís *Euboea*

Kími

Athens

Piraeus Láyrion

Ándros

Tínos

Ikaria

Pátrai

Corinth

Alfios Argos

Zante Pírgos

Peloponnesus

Kalamáta Sparta

Náxos

Cos

Rhodes

Rhodes

Líndos

Cythera Kárpathos

SEA OF CRETE

Khaniá Iráklion

Mt Ida ▲ *Crete*

(8,058 ft)

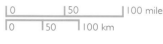
0 50 100 miles
0 50 100 km

COLOSSEUM

The Colosseum, once a large outdoor theater, is one of the best known ancient Roman ruins.

FLORENCE

The Ponte Vecchio is a bridge that spans the River Arno in the beautiful city of Florence, northern Italy.

Russia and its Neighbors

ST PETERSBURG
St Petersburg, formerly called Leningrad, is Russia's second largest city, with more than four million people.

The Soviet Union, which was also called the USSR (Union of Soviet Socialist Republics), was a Communist country. When it was dissolved in 1991, it split into 15 nations, the largest of which was Russia.

About 25 percent of Russia is in Europe, but nearly 80 percent of the Russian people live in European Russia. European Russia contains rich farmland and large cities, such as Moscow and St Petersburg. Asian Russia, or Siberia, is thinly populated, with frozen plains and windswept plateaux. But it has large oil deposits and other minerals. Of the other 14 countries formed from the Soviet Union, six – Estonia, Latvia, Lithuania, Belarus, Moldova, and Ukraine – are entirely in Europe. Three – Azerbaijan, Georgia, and Kazakhstan – lie partly in Europe but mainly in Asia, while five – Armenia, Kyrgyzstan, Tajikistan, Turkmenistan, and Uzbekistan – are entirely in Asia.

The old Communist system of political dictatorship collapsed when its economic policies failed. Today, Russia and its neighbors face many problems as they work to reform their economies and increase private ownership.

FACT FILE

● Kaliningrad is Russia's most western port. It lies between Lithuania and Poland.
● Russia lies both in Europe and Asia. It is the world's largest country, with an area of 6,592,850 sq miles (17,075,400 sq km).
● Baykonur, Kazakhstan, was the rocket launching station for the Soviet Union. After the Soviet Union broke up in 1991, Russia paid rent to Kazakhstan for the station.
● Ukraine is famous for its agriculture. It has been called the breadbasket of Europe.

MOSCOW STORE
Many goods were in short supply when Russia was ruled by Communists.

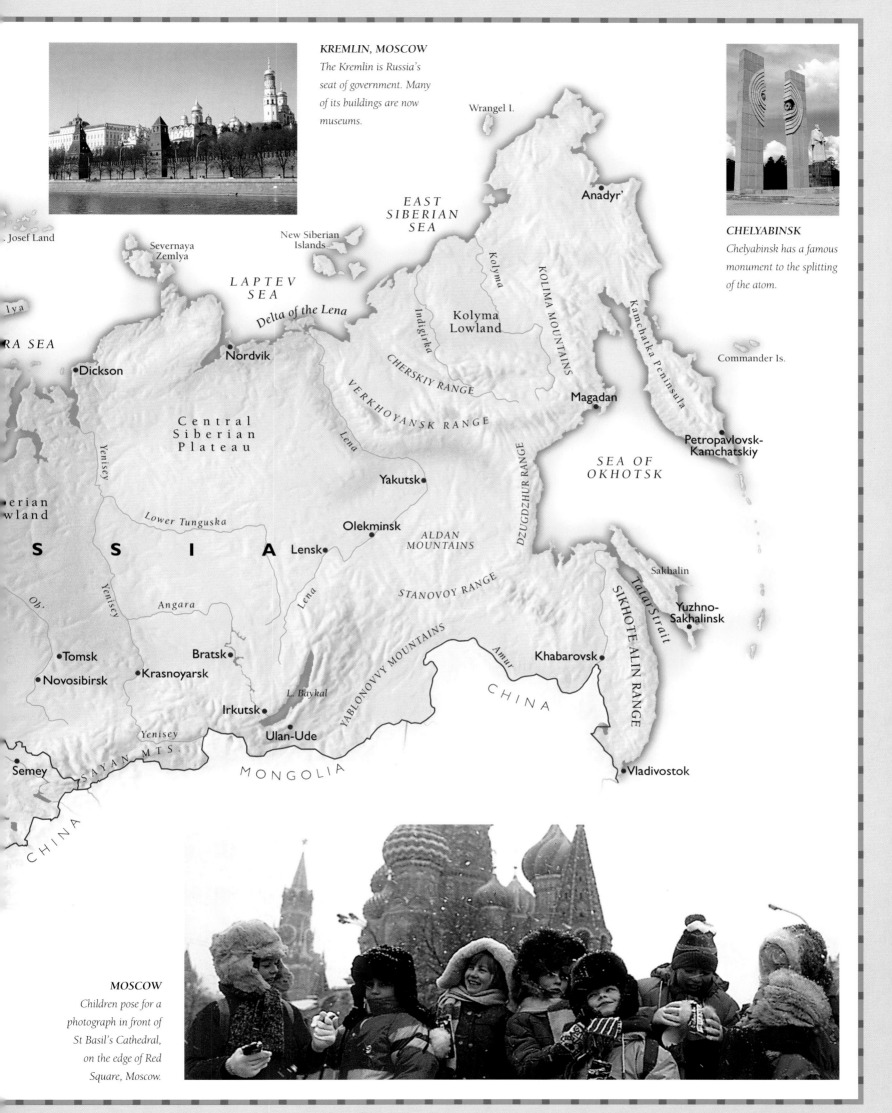

KREMLIN, MOSCOW
The Kremlin is Russia's seat of government. Many of its buildings are now museums.

Wrangel I.

EAST
SIBERIAN
SEA

Anadyr'

CHELYABINSK
Chelyabinsk has a famous monument to the splitting of the atom.

Josef Land

Severnaya
Zemlya

New Siberian
Islands

LAPTEV
SEA

Kolyma

KOLIMA MOUNTAINS

lya

RA SEA

Delta of the Lena

Commander Is.

Kamchatka Peninsula

Nordvik

Indigirka

Kolyma
Lowland

Dickson

CHERSKIY RANGE

Central
Siberian
Plateau

VERKHOYANSK RANGE

Magadan

SEA OF
OKHOTSK

Petropavlovsk-
Kamchatskiy

Yenisey

Lena

Yakutsk

DZUGDZHUR RANGE

erian
wland

Lower Tunguska

Olekminsk

ALDAN
MOUNTAINS

S S I A

Lensk

Sakhalin

Ob'

Yenisey

Lena

STANOVOY RANGE

Tatar Strait

SIKHOTE-ALIN RANGE

Yuzhno-
Sakhalinsk

Angara

YABLONOVVY MOUNTAINS

Tomsk

Bratsk

Amur

Khabarovsk

Novosibirsk

Krasnoyarsk

L. Baykal

CHINA

Irkutsk

Yenisey

Ulan-Ude

Semey

SAYAN MTS.

MONGOLIA

Vladivostok

CHINA

MOSCOW
Children pose for a photograph in front of St Basil's Cathedral, on the edge of Red Square, Moscow.

Asia

Asia is the largest of the seven continents. It covers about 30 percent of the world's land area and contains more than half of the world's people.

The continent is divided into five main regions. Northern Asia, including Asian Russia, is cold and thinly populated, with vast areas of forest, dry grasslands and cold deserts. Southwestern Asia has large areas of hot desert. It, too, is thinly populated. South-central Asia, including India, is mostly hot and wet. Many people live in the valleys of such rivers as the Indus and the Ganges. Southeastern Asia is hot and wet, with some densely populated areas. Eastern Asia, including China and Japan, has some bleak deserts in the west and north. But many people live along the coasts or in the valleys of such Chinese rivers as the Huang He and the Chang Jiang (formerly called Yangtze).

Japan is a highly developed, prosperous country. Several Asian countries have rich resources, especially oil in southwestern Asia, and some, including Singapore and South Korea, have many industries. However, many Asians are poor by comparison with people in western countries. Many live by farming, producing little more than they need to support their families.

TAJ MAHAL
The Taj Mahal, in Agra, northern India, is one of the world's most beautiful buildings. It is a major tourist attraction.

BICYCLES
In China and other developing countries of Asia, the main form of transport is the bicycle. Bicycle parks are common sights in the cities.

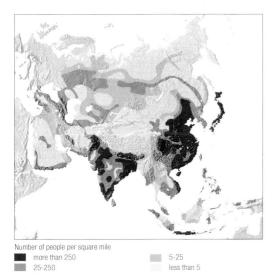

Number of people per square mile
- ■ more than 250
- ■ 25-250
- ■ 5-25
- ■ less than 5

POPULATION

Vast areas of northern Asia, including Asian Russia, are thinly populated. But parts of south-central, southeastern and eastern China are among the most crowded places in the world.

- ■ Tundra/Mountain
- ■ Northern Forest
- ■ Mixed broadleaf forest
- ■ Scrub
- ■ Grassland
- ■ Tropical Rain Forest
- ■ Tropical forest
- ■ Desert

CLIMATE

Asia stretches from the Arctic Ocean to the equator. Climates range from the Arctic north, and the harsh climates of such remote places as Tibet and the Gobi Desert, to the hot and wet climates in the south.

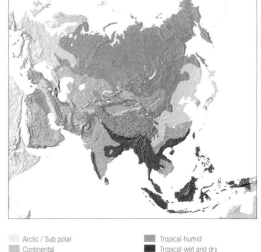

- ■ Arctic / Sub polar
- ■ Continental
- ■ Subtropical-humid
- ■ Subtropical-wet and dry
- ■ Tropical-humid
- ■ Tropical-wet and dry
- ■ Arid
- ■ High Altitude

VEGETATION

Treeless tundra regions in the north merge into huge coniferous forests. To the south lie temperate broadleaf forests, while rainforests grow in the tropical regions. Hot and cold deserts also cover large areas.

Moscow

R U S S I A

Ankara
GEORGIA
TURKEY
AZER.
ARM.
CYPRUS
LEBANON
SYRIA
ISRAEL
JORDAN
IRAQ
Baghdad

Astana

KAZAKHSTAN

UZBEKISTAN
TURKMENISTAN
KYRGYZSTAN
TAJIKISTAN

Ulan Bator
MONGOLIA

NORTH
KOREA

JAPAN
Tokyo

SOUTH
KOREA

Tehran
IRAN

AFGHANISTAN

Beijing

SAUDI
ARABIA
KUWAIT
BAHRAIN
QATAR
Riyadh
UNITED
ARAB
EMIRATES

Islamabad

PAKISTAN

C H I N A

San'a
YEMEN
Muscat
OMAN

New
Delhi
NEPAL
BHUTAN

I N D I A

BANG.

MYANMAR
(BURMA)
Yangon
(Rangoon)

LAOS
Hanoi
Vientiane

Taipei
TAIWAN

PHILIPPINE
SEA

Gulf of Aden

ARABIAN
SEA

Bay of
Bengal

THAILAND

SOUTH
CHINA
SEA

VIETNAM

Manila

PHILIPPINES

PACIFIC
OCEAN

Bangkok
CAMBODIA
Phnom
Penh

0   500   1000 miles
0   500 1000 km

SRI
LANKA
Colombo

BRUNEI

MALDIVES

M A L A Y S I A
Kuala Lumpur
SINGAPORE

INDIAN OCEAN

I N D O N E S I A

Jakarta

RICE FIELDS
Rice is the chief food crop in the hot and wet countries of south-central and southeastern Asia.

FARMING
Many people in Asia live by farming. Much of the work is done by hand.

FACT FILE
● Asia has about 3,500 million people.
● Mount Everest, the world's highest mountain, at 29,029 ft (8,848 m) above sea level, and the Dead Sea shoreline, the world's lowest point on land at 1,310 ft (400 m) below sea level, are both in Asia.
● All the world's main religions, including Buddhism, Christianity, Hinduism, Islam, Judaism, Taoism, and Shintoism, originated in Asia.

FLOATING MARKETS
Markets are meeting places for people who live in mainly farming areas. Bangkok has river markets where people in boats buy and sell their produce.

Southwest Asia

Southwestern Asia is sometimes called the Middle East. It contains hot sandy or gravel deserts, where few plants grow, together with rugged mountain ranges. Major rivers are few, except for the Tigris and Euphrates which rise in Turkey and flow into Iraq. Southwestern Asia includes Israel, a detailed map of which appears on page 36, and Turkey, which is described on page 37.

Arabs make up the majority of the people in 12 countries in this region. They include Bahrain, Kuwait, Oman, Saudi Arabia, United Arab Emirates, and Yemen, which together make up the large Arabian peninsula, together with Iraq, Jordan, Lebanon, and Syria. Israel also contains Arab citizens, called Palestinians. Cyprus is another divided country. It contains Christian Greek Cypriots and Turkish Cypriots, who are mostly Muslim.

Several countries in Southwestern Asia are rich in oil and natural gas. However, most countries lack big manufacturing industries and many people are poor farmers.

OASES

Many farmers in Southwest Asia live at oases. Oases include places where water comes to the surface, places with wells, and river valleys.

ARAB TENTS

Arabs once roamed the deserts with their herds of animals. They had few possessions and lived in tents. Today most live in permanent settlements.

FLAT BREAD

This woman practices the traditional Middle Eastern way to carry things on her head, such as this flat bread.

MUSLIM TOMB

This holy tomb is in Oman.

PETRA

Many ancient monuments, such as beautiful temples at Petra, Jordan, are found in southwestern Asia.

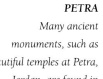

SAN'A

The Arabs consider San'a, capital of Yemen, to be the world's oldest city.

FACT FILE

- The world's oldest civilization developed at Sumer (In Southeastern Iraq) in around 3500 BC.
- Saudi Arabia has the world's largest oil reserves and is the world's leading exporter.
- The majority of people in southwest Asia are Muslims. Christians dominate in Cyprus, while most people in Israel are Jews.
- Islamic artists are forbidden to draw animals and humans. Instead, they use patterns, some of which are based on plants.

Israel

The State of Israel forms part of a historic region called Palestine. Created in 1948, it has survived wars with its Arab neighbors. Northern Israel has hot, dry summers and mild, moist winters, but the south is desert. Farmers grow many crops, including citrus fruits, but manufacturing is the leading activity.

In the 1990s, the Israeli government entered talks aimed at giving the Arab Palestinian people of Israel their own self-governing areas in the occupied Gaza Strip and West Bank. Many Palestinians hoped that they would eventually create their own country. Israelis hoped that they could achieve a peace agreement.

OLD CITY
Jerusalem has narrow old streets that seem almost unchanged from the city that existed 2,000 years ago.

FACT FILE
● Israel was created in May 1948.
● The Israelis fought wars with their Arab neighbors in 1948-9, 1956, 1967, and 1973.
● The occupied territories, including the Gaza Strip, the West Bank, and the Golan Heights, were won during Arab-Israeli wars.
● Tourism is important in Israel. Tourists visit the country's religious sites and resorts, such as Elat.
● Israel's flag contains blue and white stripes, based on a Hebrew prayer shawl, and the six-pointed Star of David.

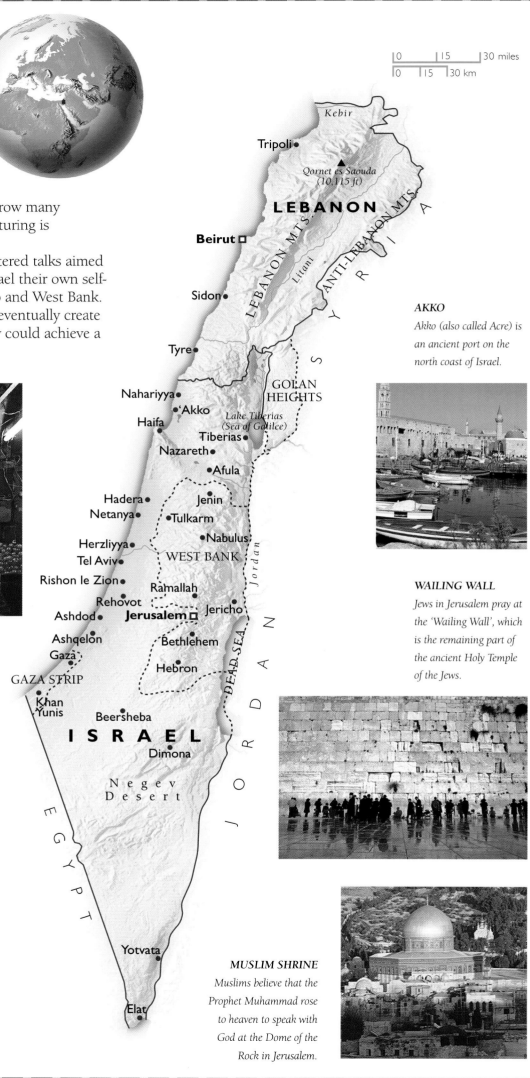

AKKO
Akko (also called Acre) is an ancient port on the north coast of Israel.

WAILING WALL
Jews in Jerusalem pray at the 'Wailing Wall', which is the remaining part of the ancient Holy Temple of the Jews.

MUSLIM SHRINE
Muslims believe that the Prophet Muhammad rose to heaven to speak with God at the Dome of the Rock in Jerusalem.

Turkey

Asian Turkey, east of the waterway that links the Black and Mediterranean seas, makes up 97 percent of the country. Most of Asian Turkey consists of rugged mountains and high plateaux. Summers are sunny and dry, but winters are cold. Farming is important and major products include barley, cotton, fruits, maize, meat, tobacco, wheat, and wool. Manufacturing is increasing.

Most people are Muslim Turks. Turkey also has a large Kurdish community. Kurds also live in Syria, Iraq, Iran, and Armenia. Many Kurds would like to have their own country and Kurdish forces have fought with troops in Turkey and elsewhere.

HOMES IN ROCKS
People have carved homes in strange rock formations in Cappadocia, a plateau near Kayseri.

ISTANBUL
The imposing Blue Mosque in Istanbul stands on a hill above the waterway that divides European and Asian Turkey.

ROCK TOMBS
From the outside, tombs carved in rock faces resemble houses and shrines, with pillars and reliefs.

FACT FILE
● Turkey lies partly in Europe and partly in Asia. The boundary between them consists of a waterway between the Black and Mediterranean seas.

● The city of Istanbul lies partly in Europe and partly in Asia. Istanbul was once called Byzantium and later Constantinople.

● Mount Ararat in eastern Turkey is supposed to be the resting place of Noah's Ark after the Biblical Flood.

● The Asian part of Turkey is also called Asia Minor or Anatolia.

South-Central Asia

In 1947, British India split to form two countries, India and Pakistan. Then, in 1971, East Pakistan became Bangladesh. South-central Asia also includes Bhutan and Nepal in the north, and Sri Lanka (formerly Ceylon) and the Maldives in the south.

Great rivers, including the Indus and Ganges, flow from the Himalaya range in the north. The region also includes the Great Indian (or Thar) Desert on the India-Pakistan border, and the Deccan plateau in southern India. South-central Asia has a tropical climate. Most people are poor farmers and rice is the chief crop. But manufacturing industries are increasing in India and Pakistan.

TAJ MAHAL
The magnificent Taj Mahal, Agra, was erected by an Indian ruler between 1630 and 1650 as a tomb for his wife.

ANCIENT FORT
India has many ancient forts, temples, and other buildings that attract visitors from all over the world.

BENGAL TIGER
This beautiful animal is now an endangered species.

HEADGEAR
Turbans are worn by many people in Hindu and Muslim countries.

FACT FILE

● India is the seventh largest country, but only China has more people than India.
● The world's largest delta has been formed by the Ganges and Brahmaputra rivers.
● The world's most destructive cyclone (circular storm) killed around a million people in Bangladesh in 1970.
● The Indus valley civilization developed in what is now Pakistan and northwest India around 4,500 years ago.

CATTLE *India has more cattle than any other country. Hindus do not kill cattle for their meat, but they drink cows' milk.*

Andaman Is.

Andaman
&
Nicobar Is.
(India)

Nicobar Is.

Map labels

AFGHANISTAN
IRAN
KARAKORAM
K2 (28,251 ft)
Peshawar
Islamabad
Srinagar
Rawalpindi
Lahore
Quetta
Faisalabad
Amritsar
PAKISTAN
Multan
Sukkur Bahawalpur
Indus
Great Indian Desert (Thar Desert)
Nanda Devi (25,646 ft)
Tibet (CHINA)
Delhi
New Delhi
NEPAL
Mt Annapurna (26,503 ft)
Mt Everest (29,029 ft)
Thimphu
BHUTAN
Hyderabad
Bareilly
Katmandu
Karachi
Jodhpur
Jaipur
Agra
Lucknow
Ghagara
Brahmaputra
Ajmer
Kanpur
Varanasi
Guwahati
Udaipur
Kota
Allahabad
Ganges
Patna
NAGA HILLS
Ahmadabad
Indore
Bhopal
Son
Asanol
BANGLADESH
Dhaka
Imphal
Jamnagar
Vadodara
Narmada
Jabalpur
Jamshedpur
Khulna
MYANMAR (BURMA)
Bhavnagar Surat
INDIA
Kolkata (Calcutta)
Chittagong
ARABIAN SEA
Gulf of Khambhat
Aurangabad
Nagpur
Raipur
Mahanadi
Cuttack
Mouths of the Ganges
Mumbai (Bombay)
Deccan
Godavari
Pune
Solapur
Hyderabad
GHATS
Bay of Bengal
Kolhapur
WESTERN GHATS
Krishna
Vishakhapatnam
Kurnool
EASTERN
Vijayawada
Penner
Nellore
Mangalore
Bangalore
Chennai (Madras)
Mysore
Kozhikode
Coimbatore
Cochin Madurai
Jaffna
Trivandrum
Trincomalee
Gulf of Mannar
SRI LANKA
Kandy
Colombo
Galle
INDIAN OCEAN

Scale

0 200 400 miles
0 100 400 km

Southeast Asia

Southeast Asia includes several countries which form a peninsula jutting south from the Asian mainland. They include Cambodia, Laos, and Vietnam, which were once ruled by France, Myanmar (which was formerly British and called Burma), and Thailand, the only Southeast Asian country that was never ruled by a foreign power.

The north is mountainous, with lowlands in the south. The chief river is the Mekong, which reaches the sea in southeastern Vietnam. The climate is tropical and most people are poor farmers. In the last 30 years, Thailand has greatly increased its manufacturing industries and its tourist industry has grown quickly.

FACT FILE
● Thailand was once called Siam; Myanmar was called Burma, and Cambodia was called the Khmer Republic and Kampuchea.
● Myanmar is one of the world's leading producers of rubies.
● Thai boxers use their feet as well as their fists to strike their opponent.
● A civil war occurred in Vietnam between 1957 and 1975.

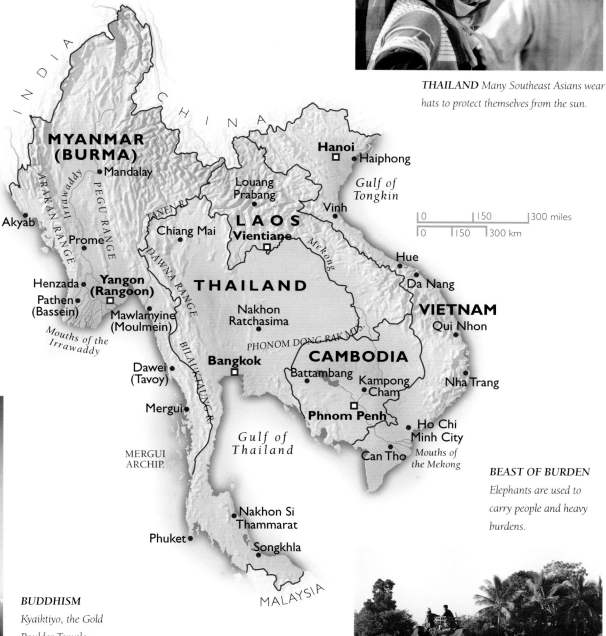

THAILAND *Many Southeast Asians wear hats to protect themselves from the sun.*

OX CART
Traditional methods of transport are used in Myanmar and the rest of southeastern Asia.

BEAST OF BURDEN
Elephants are used to carry people and heavy burdens.

BUDDHISM
Kyaiktiyo, the Gold Boulder Temple, celebrates Buddhism, the chief religion of Myanmar.

Southeast Asia (2)

Southeast Asia also includes three island countries – Indonesia, the Philippines, and Singapore. It also includes Malaysia, which lies partly on mainland Asia, and has two provinces, Sabah and Sarawak, on the island of Borneo. Also on Borneo is the oil-rich Islamic Sultanate of Brunei.

Indonesia and the Philippines lie in unstable parts of our planet. Indonesia has more active volcanoes than any other country in the world, and volcanic eruptions and earthquakes are also common in the Philippines. The climate is tropical and rainforests cover large areas. However, much of the original forest has been destroyed to make way for farms. Apart from Singapore. which is a small but prosperous country with many industries, Southeast Asia is a developing region. Agriculture employs nearly 60 percent of the people and many of them are poor. Rice is the chief food crop, while other crops grown for export include cocoa, coconuts, coffee, and tea. However, in the last 30 years, manufacturing has increased rapidly in Indonesia, Malaysia and the Philippines.

DANCING *Traditional dancers in Indonesia wear elaborate and intricately embellished costumes.*

FACT FILE

● Singapore is densely populated, with more than 13,000 people per sq mile (5,000 people per sq km).
● Rice terraces built like steps down steep slopes in the northern Philippines were constructed more than 2,000 years ago.
● The sound of a volcanic explosion in 1883 on the small island of Krakatoa, between Sumatra and Java, Indonesia, was heard as far away as Cambodia and Australia.
● The Philippines is the only large Asian country where most people are Christians.
● Indonesia contains more Muslims than any other country in the world.
● People in the prosperous, oil-rich Sultanate of Brunei pay no income tax.

SINGAPORE

Singapore is an independent city-state and a major port.

FESTIVALS

Colorful parades are held during festivals in Singapore.

PHILIPPINES

Bamboo is a building material in the Philippines.

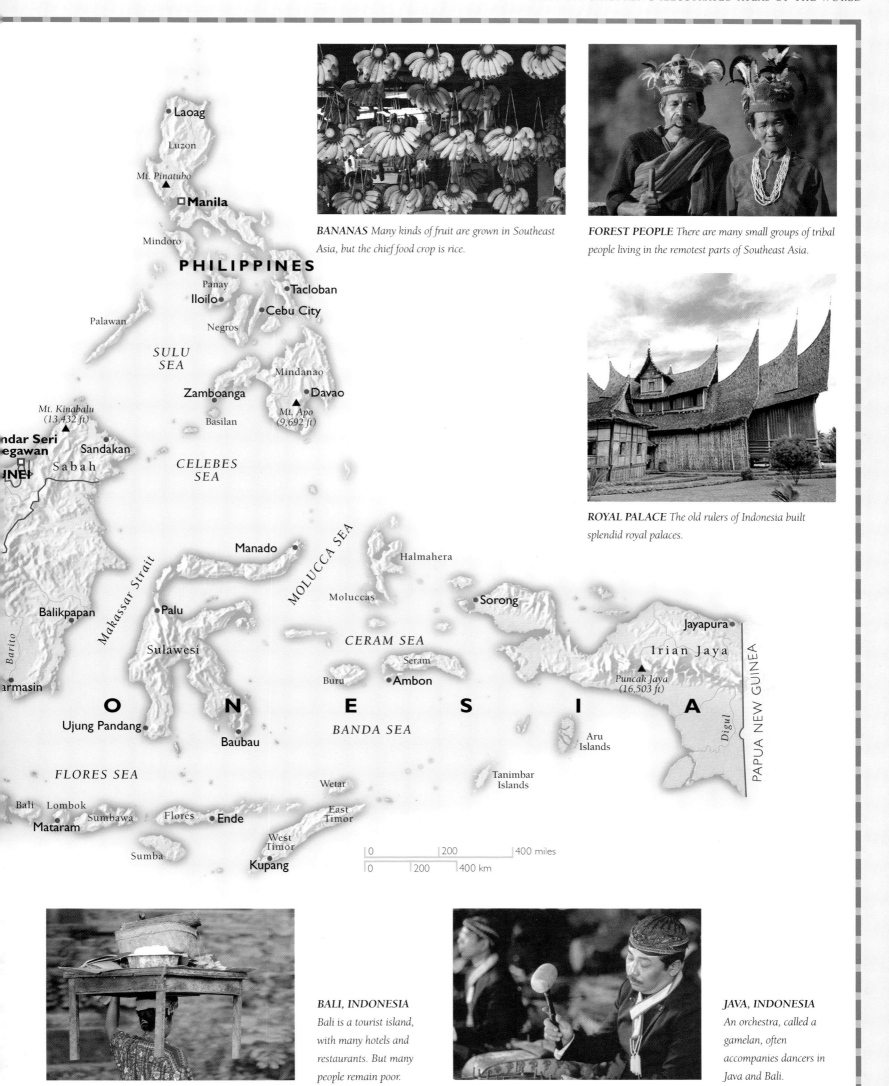

BANANAS *Many kinds of fruit are grown in Southeast Asia, but the chief food crop is rice.*

FOREST PEOPLE *There are many small groups of tribal people living in the remotest parts of Southeast Asia.*

ROYAL PALACE *The old rulers of Indonesia built splendid royal palaces.*

Laoag

Luzon

Mt. Pinatubo ▲

□ **Manila**

Mindoro

PHILIPPINES

Panay

Iloilo ●

● **Tacloban**

Palawan

Negros

● **Cebu City**

SULU SEA

Mindanao

Zamboanga

● **Davao**

Mt. Kinabalu
(13,432 ft) ▲

Basilan

Mt. Apo
(9,692 ft) ▲

ndar Seri
egawan

Sandakan

CELEBES SEA

NEI

Sabah

Manado ●

MOLUCCA SEA

Halmahera

Moluccas

● **Sorong**

Jayapura ●

Balikpapan ●

Palu ●

CERAM SEA

Seram

Irian Jaya

Barito

Sulawesi

Buru

● Ambon

Puncak Jaya
(16,503 ft) ▲

Makassar Strait

O N E S I A

PAPUA NEW GUINEA

armasin

Ujung Pandang ●

BANDA SEA

Aru
Islands

Digul

Baubau

FLORES SEA

Wetar

Tanimbar
Islands

Bali   Lombok

Sumbawa   Flores   ● **Ende**

East
Timor

Mataram

Sumba

West
Timor

Kupang

| 0 | 200 | 400 miles |
| 0 | 200 | 400 km |

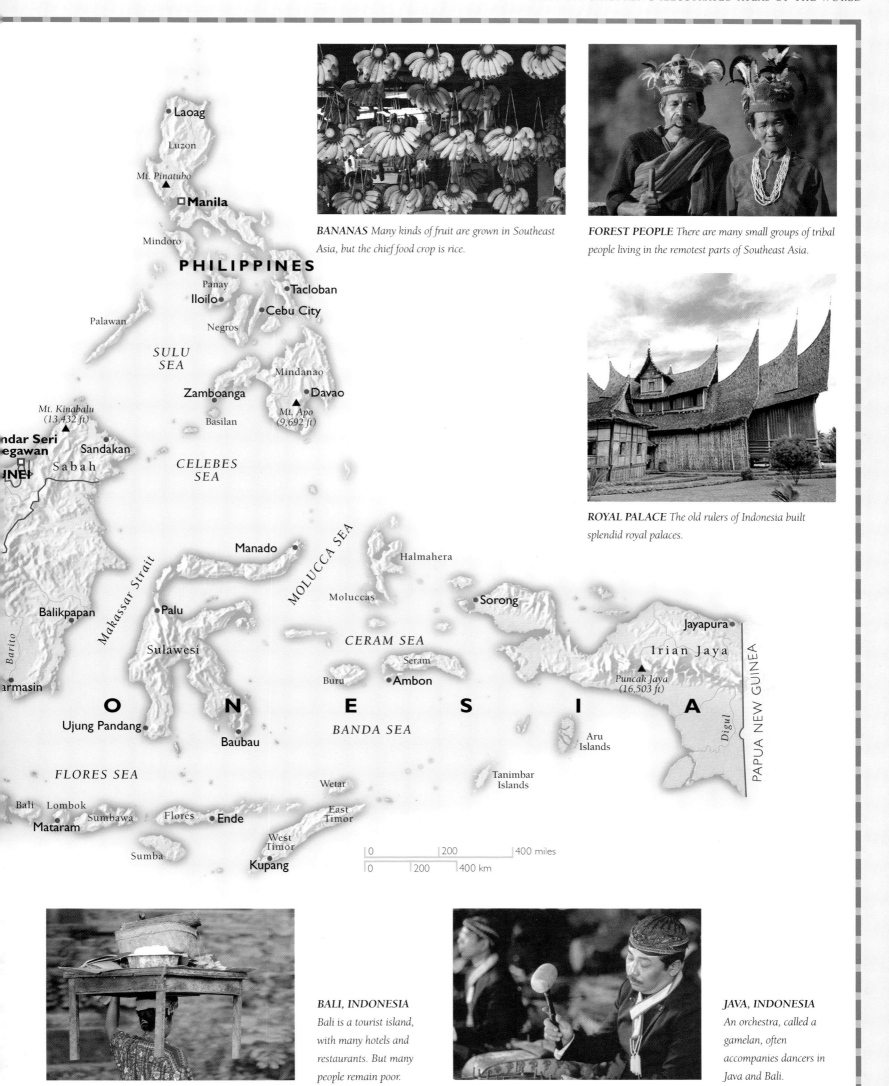

BALI, INDONESIA *Bali is a tourist island, with many hotels and restaurants. But many people remain poor.*

JAVA, INDONESIA *An orchestra, called a gamelan, often accompanies dancers in Java and Bali.*

East Asia

East Asia includes Communist China, the world's third largest country, and Japan, a great economic power. Also included are Mongolia, between China and Russia, Communist North Korea and the more prosperous South Korea, which occupy the Korean peninsula, and Taiwan. The Chinese regard Taiwan as part of China, but the Taiwanese have their own non-Communist government. Hong Kong, a former British territory on China's southeast coast, was returned to China in 1997, though it has kept much of its economic independence. Nearby is Macao, which Portugal agreed to return to China in 1999.

About 70 percent of China's people work on farms, as compared with 7 percent in Japan, with its great industrial cities. But manufacturing is increasing rapidly in eastern China, and also in South Korea and Taiwan. Japan imports food, but China is a major farming country. Its crops include rice, sweet potatoes, tea, and wheat.

GREAT WALL OF CHINA
This famous wall was built to hold back northern invaders.

GIANT PANDA
This endangered animal is found in southwestern and western China.

FACT FILE

● China has a population of 1,227,177,000.
● The world's most destructive earthquake occurred in Japan in 1923. About 575 homes were destroyed in Tokyo and Yokohama.
● The Chang Jiang (formerly Yangtze River) in China is the world's third longest river at 3,915 miles (6,300 km).
● The Korean peninsula contains two countries: Communist North Korea and democratic South Korea.
● The Great Wall of China has a total length of 4,600 miles (7,400 km).

BICYCLES
Bicycles and bicycle-drawn carts are common sights in China's cities, including the capital, Beijing.

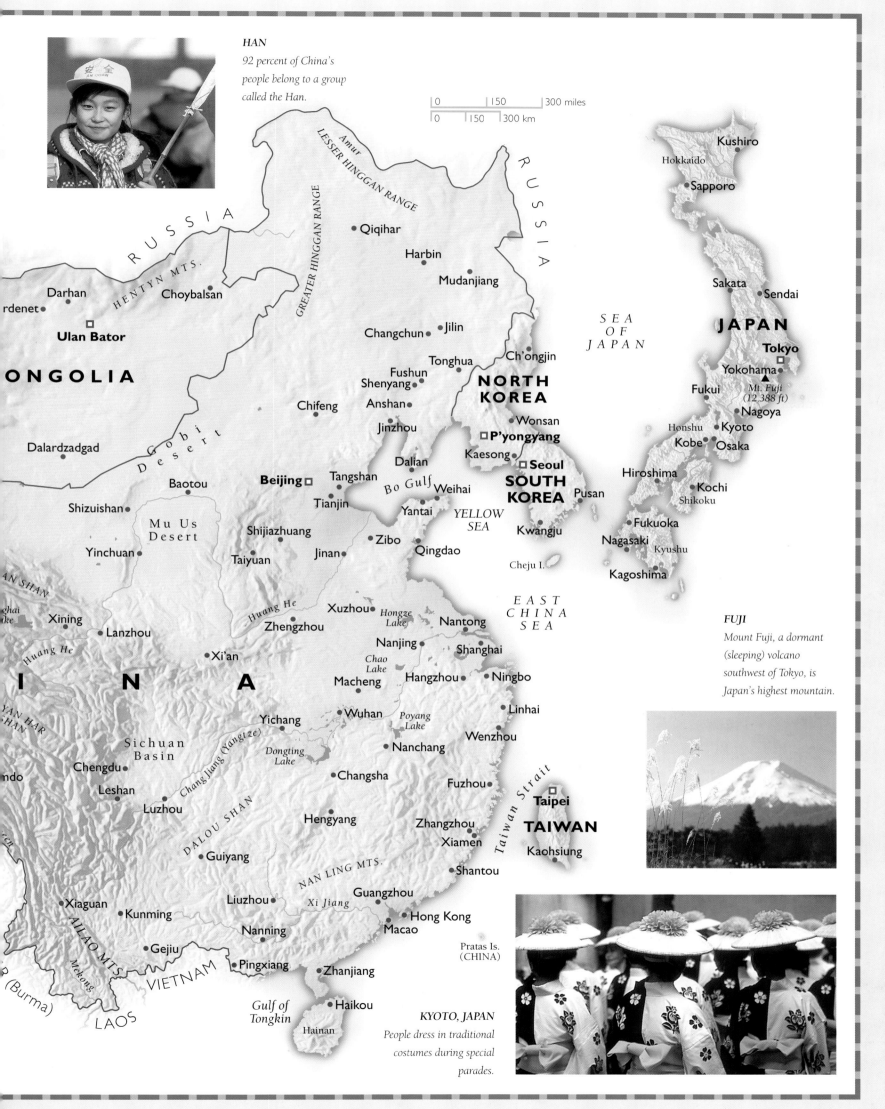

HAN

92 percent of China's people belong to a group called the Han.

0   150   300 miles
0   150   300 km

RUSSIA

Amur

LESSER HINGGAN RANGE

GREATER HINGGAN RANGE

RUSSIA

Kushiro

Hokkaido

Sapporo

Qiqihar

Harbin

Mudanjiang

HENTYN MTS.

Darhan   Choybalsan

rdenet

☐ **Ulan Bator**

ONGOLIA

Changchun   Jilin

Ch'ongjin

Tonghua

Fushun
Shenyang

NORTH KOREA

Sakata

Sendai

SEA OF JAPAN

JAPAN

☐ **Tokyo**

Yokohama
▲ Mt. Fuji
(12,388 ft)

Fukui

Nagoya

Anshan

Jinzhou

Wonsan

☐ **P'yongyang**

Kaesong

Dalian

☐ **Seoul**

Chifeng

Dalardzadgad

Gobi Desert

Baotou

Shizuishan

Mu Us Desert

Yinchuan

Beijing ☐

Tangshan

Tianjin

Shijiazhuang

Taiyuan

Bo Gulf

Weihai

Yantai

SOUTH KOREA

Pusan

Honshu

Kyoto

Kobe

Osaka

Hiroshima

Kochi

Shikoku

AN SHAN

ghai
ke

Xining

Lanzhou

Huang He

Jinan

Zibo

Qingdao

YELLOW SEA

Kwangju

Cheju I.

Fukuoka

Nagasaki

Kyushu

Kagoshima

Huang He

Xi'an

Xuzhou

Hongze
Lake

Nantong

EAST CHINA SEA

INA

Zhengzhou

Nanjing

Shanghai

FUJI

Mount Fuji, a dormant (sleeping) volcano southwest of Tokyo, is Japan's highest mountain.

Sichuan Basin

Macheng

Chao Lake

Hangzhou

Ningbo

Chengdu

Yichang

Chang Jiang (Yangtze)

Wuhan

Dongting Lake

Poyang Lake

Nanchang

Linhai

Leshan

Luzhou

DALOU SHAN

Changsha

Wenzhou

Hengyang

Fuzhou

Zhangzhou

Taiwan Strait

☐ **Taipei**

YAN HAR
shan

ndo

en

Xiaguan

Kunming

AILAO MTS

Guiyang

NAN LING MTS.

Liuzhou

Xi Jiang

Xiamen

Kaohsiung

TAIWAN

Shantou

Guangzhou

Nanning

Hong Kong
Macao

Pratas Is.
(CHINA)

R (Burma)

Mekong

Gejiu

Pingxiang

Zhanjiang

VIETNAM

LAOS

Gulf of Tongkin

Haikou

Hainan

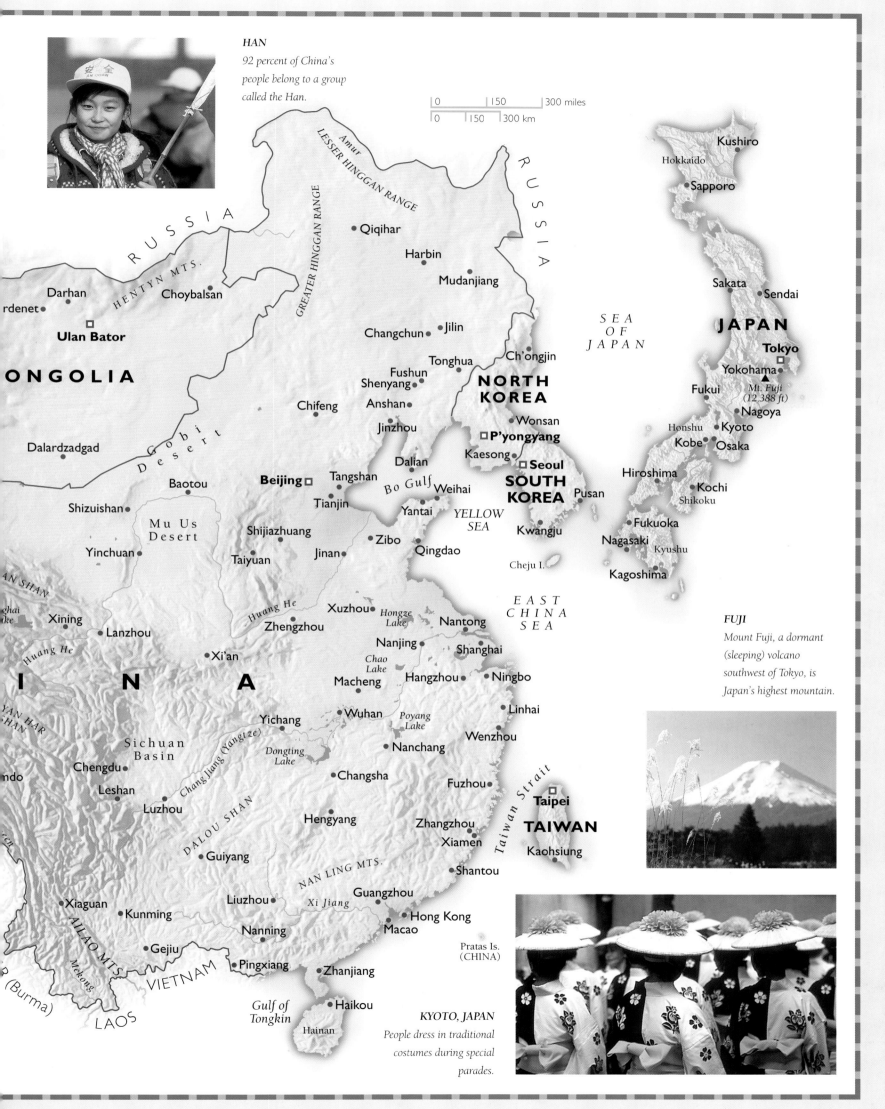

FUJI

KYOTO, JAPAN

People dress in traditional costumes during special parades.

Africa

A frica, the second largest continent, covers about a fifth of the world's land area. But large areas are covered by sparsely-populated deserts and rainforests. The equator runs through central Africa and much of the land lies in the tropics. As a result, it is the hottest continent. Rainfall is plentiful in central Africa, but deserts lie to the north and south. The continent contains 53 independent countries. This includes six island nations: Madagascar, Cape Verde off the west coast of Africa, São Tomé and Príncipe in west-central Africa, the Comoros at the north end of the Mozambique Channel, and Mauritius and the Seychelles in the Indian Ocean.

Many African countries are poor. About 60 percent of the people depend on farming, as compared with 3 percent in the United States. But many African farmers work the land by hand and they struggle to support their families. When droughts or other disasters strike, the people starve. Africa also faces political problems. About 50 years ago, European powers ruled most of Africa. In the years after independence, military dictators and one-party rulers seized control in many countries. But many Africans now believe that the best way to raise living standards is through democratic government.

SAHARA

The Sahara desert covers about 30 percent of Africa. It contains areas of sand, gravel and bare rock.

ISLAM

This mosque is in Mali. Most North Africans are Muslims.

HOMES

Thatched houses are common in Africa south of the Sahara.

Rabat

MOROCCO

ALGE

Western Sahara

MAURITANIA

Nouakchott

MALI

SENEGAL
Dakar
GAMBIA
Banjul
Bissau
GUINEA-BISSAU
Conakry
Freetown
SIERRA LEONE

Bamako

Ouagadougou
BURKINA FASO

Nian

GUINEA

Monrovia
LIBERIA

CÔTE
D'IVOIRE

Yamoussoukro

GHANA
TOGO
BENIN

Lome
Accra
Porto
Novo

Gulf of Guinea

ATLANTIC OCEAN

EQUATOR

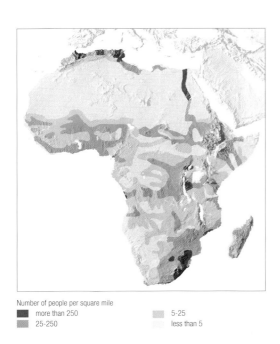

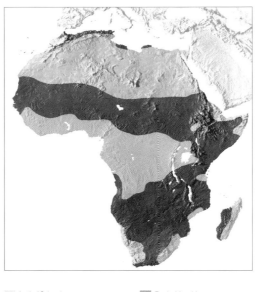

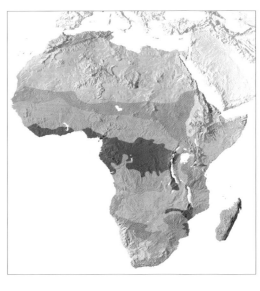

Number of people per square mile
- more than 250
- 25-250
- 5-25
- less than 5

- Arctic / Sub polar
- Continental
- Subtropical-humid
- Subtropical-wet and dry
- Tropical-humid
- Tropical-wet and dry
- A'id
- High Altitude

- Tundra/Mountain
- Northern Forest
- Mixed broadleaf forest
- Scrub
- Grassland
- Tropical Rain Forest
- Tropical forest
- Desert

POPULATION

Many people live in northwestern Africa and also in the Nile valley in Egypt. South of the Sahara, densely populated areas occur in West Africa, the East African highlands and South Africa.

CLIMATE

Climates range from the subtropical, Mediterranean type in the far north and south to the tropical humid climates, with their heavy rainfall, near the equator. The plateaus are cooler than the coasts.

VEGETATION

The tropical rainforests, with rain throughout the year, merge into tropical grasslands (savanna) in areas with a dry season. In turn, the savanna merges into dry scrub and eventually desert.

ELEPHANTS

Elephants, the largest land animals, live in the savanna and forests of Africa.

LIONS

Lions are Africa's most famous predators. The continent's wildlife attracts many tourists.

FACT FILE

● Africa has a population of approximately 734 million. Of the 53 independent countries, Nigeria, with 117,897,000 people, has the largest population.

● Sudan is Africa's largest country, with an area of 967,500 sq miles (2,505,813 sq km).

● More than 800 languages are spoken in Africa. To communicate with others, many Africans speak several languages.

● The Sahara, with an area of about 3.5 million sq miles (9 million sq km), is the world's largest desert.

ZEBRAS *Zebras share a water hole with elephants. During the dry season in the African savanna, water holes often dry up.*

HOMESTEADS

Such houses in South Africa reflect the influence of European rule.

SOUTH AFRICA

The end of apartheid (racial discrimination) in 1994 has offered hope to young South Africans.

MEDITERRANEAN SEA

ers
Tunis
TUNISIA
Tripoli

LIBYA

Cairo

EGYPT

RED SEA

N G E R

CHAD

Khartoum

Asmera
ERITREA

N'Djaména

SUDAN

DJIBOUTI
Djibouti

ERIA
buja

Addis Ababa

SOMALIA

**CENTRAL
AFRICAN
REPUBLIC**

ETHIOPIA

CAMEROON

Bangui

EA
Libreville

Yaoundé

O

UGANDA

Mogadishu

KENYA

GABON

**REPUBLIC
OF
CONGO**

Kampala

**DEMOCRATIC
REPUBLIC
OF
CONGO
(ZAIRE)**

Nairobi

RWANDA
Kigali

Brazzaville

Kinshasa

BURUNDI
Bujumbura

Dodoma

TANZANIA

Luanda

SEYCHELLES

ANGOLA

COMOROS
Moroni

*INDIAN
OCEAN*

MALAWI

ZAMBIA

Lilongwe

Lusaka

Harare

MOZAMBIQUE

Mozambique Channel

Antananarivo

MAURITIUS

NAMIBIA

ZIMBABWE

MADAGASCAR

Réunion
(France)

Port
Louis

Windhoek

BOTSWANA

Gaborone

Pretoria
Maputo
Mbabane
SWAZILAND

Maseru

**SOUTH
AFRICA**

LESOTHO

Cape Town

KROMDRAAI CASH STORE

| 0 | 250 | 500 miles |
| 0 | 250 | 500 km |

North and West Africa

SOLDIERS
Morocco is the only monarchy in North and West Africa. Most of its soldiers are fine horsemen.

Arabs from Arabia invaded North Africa in the 7th century AD. They introduced Arabic and the Islamic religion. In the Middle Ages, Arab traders visited West African empires, such as ancient Ghana and ancient Mali. Gradually, Arabs converted many people in West Africa to Islam. However, many still followed ancient African beliefs, while others became Christians in the 19th and 20th centuries.

The Muslim, Arabic-speaking countries of North Africa are richer than those to the south of the Sahara. Algeria and Libya produce oil and natural gas, and Morocco mines phosphate rock, which is used to make fertilizers. Egypt has some oil and is Africa's second most industrialized country after South Africa. Many people in West Africa are poor. Nigeria exports oil and has been developing industries. However, its progress has been hampered by the rule of military dictators. Farming employs about 55 percent of the people of West Africa.

HOUSES
Most village houses in West Africa are made of timber and dried mud.

FACT FILE

● Ancient Egypt became powerful when Upper and Lower Egypt united in 3100 BC.
● Western Sahara is occupied by Morocco, but some local people would like Western Sahara to become a separate country.
● Gambia is mainland Africa's smallest country. It occupies the Gambia river valley.
● The Nile, the world's longest river, rises in East Africa and flows 4,145 miles (6,670 km) to the Mediterranean Sea.
● Cairo, capital of Egypt, is Africa's largest city, with a population of 6,452,000.

IVORY COAST *Farming supports about 60 percent of the people. Abidjan has factories that process farm products.*

MALI *Medieval African empires in what is now Mali traded with Arabs from the north. Many people became Muslims.*

CAMELS

Because they can go long distances without water, camels are important beasts of burden in North Africa.

STATUES

The towering statues at Abu Simbel in southern Egypt are examples of ancient Egyptian art.

SPHINX

The Great Sphinx, close to the pyramids near Cairo, Egypt, has a human head and a lion's body.

M E D I T E R R A N E A N   S E A

nnaba
stantine □ **Tunis**
TUNISIA • Sfax

Darnah

• Ghadamis **Tripoli** • Misurata Benghazi

L I B Y A

r a

Libyan Desert

Alexandria Port Said
Qattara **Cairo** • Suez
Depression Sinai
Pen.
ISRAEL

• Asyût Nile

Luxor

E G Y P T

• Aswân

L. Nasser

R E D S E A

TIBESTI
MTS.

Emi Koussi
(11,204 ft)

• Faya-Largeau

Nubian
Desert

• Merowe Port Sudan

Nile

GER

CHAD

Bodélé
Depression

S U D A N

• Atbara

• Kassala

Kano • Maiduguri
ria

• L. Chad • Abéché

□ **N'Djaména**

Jabal Marrah
(10,131 ft)

Omdurman
Khartoum • El Obeid

• Kosti

Blue Nile Atbara

ETHIOPIA

ERITREA

Chari

Benue Yola
• Garoua • Sarh
RIA

CENTRAL AFRICAN REPUBLIC

Sudd

White Nile

CAMEROON

• Douala □ **Yaoundé**

NEA GABON

REP. OF
CONGO

DEM. REP. OF
CONGO

Nimule

UGANDA

0   200   400 miles
0   200   400 km

DOGON VILLAGE

Most of the Dogon people of Mali live in villages with round houses. The towers are used to store grain.

BERBERS

Berbers lived throughout North Africa before the arrival of the Arabs. Today, many Berbers live in villages.

East Africa

East Africa consists mainly of high plateaus, which are cooler than the hot, humid coastal plains. The region contains deserts, rainforest, and large areas of scrub and tropical savanna, which support many wild animals. Several countries have national parks to protect the animals.

Ethiopia was an ancient Christian empire until its emperor was overthrown in 1974. The rest of East Africa was ruled by European powers from the late 19th century until the early 1960s. Since then, the countries have struggled to raise living standards and they rank among the world's 25 poorest. Civil war has occurred in many areas.

LIONS
The scrub and tropical grassland of East Africa support many grazing animals, which are hunted by lions.

GORILLAS
The mountain gorilla in the forests of western East Africa is an endangered species.

GIRAFFES *The national parks of Kenya and Tanzania attract many tourists to see wildlife in its natural state.*

KILIMANJARO
Africa's highest mountain overlooks tropical plains with herds of wild animals.

FACT FILE

● Kilimanjaro, at 19,341 ft (5,895 m) above sea level, is Africa's highest mountain.
● Ethiopia has been a Christian nation since the 4th century AD.
● The Hutu and Tutsi people of Burundi and Rwanda have fought each other in recent years, causing many lives to be lost.
● Lake Victoria, which covers 26,828 sq miles (69.484 sq km), is Africa's largest lake.
● Part of the Great Rift Valley, which extends from Mozambique, through the Red Sea, to Syria, runs through East Africa.

RED SEA

ERITREA
□ Asmara
● Aksum
▲ Ras Dashen (15,158 ft)
Gonder ●
L. Tana
Debre Markos ●
Blue Nile
DJIBOUTI
□ Djibouti   Gulf of Aden
Berbera ●
Dire Dawa ●
Addis Ababa □
Gore ● ETHIOPIA
Jima ●   Webe Shebele   Ogaden

SUDAN

Rift Valley

SOMALIA

L. Turkana

UGANDA
L. Albert
Kampala ▲ □
Margherita Peak (18,737 ft)
Juba
KENYA
Kisumu ●
Mt. Kenya ▲ (17,057 ft)
● Meru
Mogadishu □
Kismayu ●
INDIAN OCEAN

RWANDA
□ Kigali
Bukavu ●
L. Victoria
□ Nairobi
Bujumbura ●
BURUNDI
● Mwanza
Voi ●
Tana
Tabora ●
▲ Kilimanjaro 19,341 ft
Mombasa ●
Tanga ●
Dodoma ●
Zanzibar ●
L. Tanganyika
ZAMBIA
Rufiji
Dar-es-Salaam ●
L. Rukwa
TANZANIA
● Mbeya
L. Nyasa
Mtwara ●
MALAWI
● Songea
MOZAMBIQUE

0   150   300 miles
0   150   300 km

EDUCATION
Most East African children get basic primary schooling. High School is only for a minority.

Central and Southern Africa

Much of Central and Southern Africa consists of high plateaus. It contains rainforests in the north, deserts in the southwest, together with scrub and grassland, populated by wild animals.

The region includes Africa's third largest country, the Democratic Republic of Congo (formerly called Zaire). This country has rich mineral deposits, including copper and diamonds, but most people are farmers. South Africa is Africa's most developed country. It produces diamonds, gold and other minerals and its many factories manufacture a wide range of products. However, until 1994, black Africans were not allowed to vote under a system of racial discrimination called apartheid.

SPRINGBOKS
These antelopes were once common in Southern Africa.

ROUGH TERRAIN
Many parts of Southern africa are only accessible with a four wheel drive vehicle.

FACT FILE

● The Democratic Republic of Congo was called Zaire between 1971 and 1997. Before it became independent in 1960, it was known as the Belgian Congo.
● South Africa has 11 official languages: Afrikaans, English, Ndebele, North Sotho, South Sotho, Swazi, Tsonga, Tswana, Venda, Xhosa, and Zulu.
● The Victoria Falls is also called Mosi oa Tunya, meaning 'the smoke that thunders'.
● Madagascar and the Comoro Islands are the only places to have lemurs.

WINE MAKING
Southwestern South Africa is a leading producer of wines.

CAPE TOWN
This South African city is overlooked by Table Mountain.

Oceania

Oceania consists of Australia, the world's sixth largest country, and the Pacific islands. The Pacific islands are divided into three groups. Melanesia means 'dark islands'. Its name comes from the dark skins of the people, such as those in Papua New Guinea. Micronesia means 'small islands'. It includes the tiny islands north of Melanesia, including those in the Federated States of Micronesia and the Marshall Islands. Finally, Polynesia means 'many islands'. It includes most of the islands within a triangle formed by the Midway Islands in the north, Easter Island in the southeast, and New Zealand in the southwest.

Some islands are high and rugged. They are volcanoes, whose slopes are often covered by tropical forests. By contrast, the low islands are made of coral, which has piled up on top of submerged or sinking volcanoes. Many islands have beautiful beaches cooled by fresh ocean breezes. Many islands are tourist resorts.

Number of people per square mile

■ more than 250	■ 5-25
■ 25-250	☐ less than 5

POPULATION

Australia has a population of approximately 18,532,000. Most people live in the southeast, and the rest of Australia is desolate. New Zealand has a population of 3,761,000 and the other Pacific islands about 7.3 million.

CORAL ISLAND

Many low-lying Pacific islands are made of the external limestone skeletons of tiny animals, called coral polyps.

TOURISTS

Many islands have spectacular sandy beaches surrounded by palm trees, making them ideal as tourist resorts.

HAWAII (U.S.A.)

Johnston Atoll
(U.S.A.)

S O U T H
P A C I F I C
O C E A N

Howland
(U.S.A.)

Baker (U.S.A.)

K I R I B A T I

TUVALU

Tokelau Is.
(N.Z.)

Marquesas Is.

SAMOA

Wallis & Futuna
(France)

American
Samoa
(U.S.A)

FIJI

Niue
(N.Z.)

Cook
Islands
(N.Z.)

French
Polynesia

TONGA

Pitcairn Is.
(U.K.)

Kermadec Is.
(N.Z.)

Easter Island
(Chile)

0   500   1000 miles
0   500   1000 km

NEW
ZEALAND

Auckland

North I.

Wellington

Chatham Is.
(N.Z.)

Christchurch

th I.

FACT FILE

● About 60 percent of Australia's population live in five cities: Sydney, Melbourne, Brisbane, Perth, and Adelaide.
● New Zealand's first people, the Maoris, arrived there more than 1,000 years ago.
● More than 740 languages are spoken in Papua New Guinea.
● No one knows how many islands are in the Pacific Ocean. Estimates range from 20,000 to more than 30,000.

PINE TREES The Isle of Pines is in New Caledonia, a French overseas territory.

MARQUESAN BOY The Marquesas are a group of islands in French Polynesia.

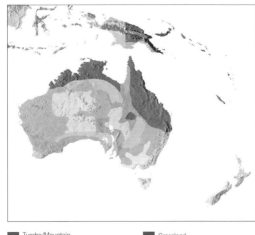

Tundra/Mountain
Northern Forest
Mixed broadleaf forest
Scrub
Grassland
Tropical Rain Forest
Tropical forest
Desert

VEGETATION

Oceania has many vegetation types, ranging from tropical forests in northern Australia and many Pacific islands, to deserts, scrub and subtropical forests, including eucalyptus (or gum tree) forests in Australia.

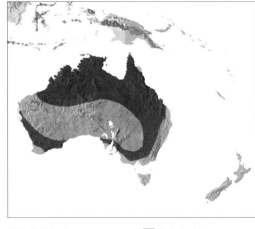

Arctic / Sub polar
Continental
Subtropical-humid
Subtropical-wet and dry
Tropical-humid
Tropical-wet and dry
Arid
High Altitude

CLIMATE

Australia is tropical in the north, arid in the west and subtropical in the populated southeast. Much of New Zealand has a mild, rainy climate, but most Pacific islands are in the tropics and are always warm.

PALM TREES

pbell Is.
N.Z.)

Large numbers of coconut palms grow on many islands in the Pacific Ocean. Copra, the dried meat of coconuts, and coconut oil are major products throughout the Pacific.

Australia

Australia is the only country which is also a continent. The Great Dividing Range separates the eastern coastal plains from the central lowlands, which contain vast cattle and sheep ranches. Australia's longest rivers, the Murray and the Darling, drain the southeastern lowlands. Lake Eyre is Australia's largest lake, but it is dry for most of the year. The western plateau is largely desert.

About 58 percent of Australia is used for pasture and 6 percent is used for crops. Australia is a major producer of farm products. It is rich in minerals and its cities contain many factories.

FACT FILE
● Australia's highest peak is Mount Kosciuszko in the southeast.
● The Great Barrier Reef, the world's longest group of coral reefs, extends about 1,250 miles (2,010 km) along the northeast coast of Australia.
● The Aboriginal name for Ayers Rock in Northern Territory is Uluru, which means 'great pebble'.
● The name Australia comes from a Latin word Australis, meaning 'southern'.
● Australia is the flattest continent.

0   200   400 miles
0   200   400 km

KOALAS

Koalas are Australian mammals that live on the leaves and young shoots of eucalyptus trees.

KANGAROOS

Many Australian animals, including koalas, wallabies and kangaroos, are marsupials.

ULURU

Northern Territory contains Uluru (or Ayers Rock), one of Australia's natural wonders.

THE OUTBACK

People travel long distances to explore the outback (interior) of Australia.

New Zealand

New Zealand consists of two large islands and several much smaller ones. North Island contains active volcanoes and spectacular geysers. But South Island's Southern Alps contain the country's highest peak, Mount Cook. The climate is warm and humid at Auckland, New Zealand's largest city, in the far north. To the south, the climate becomes cooler. Temperatures sometimes fall below freezing in winter at Dunedin in the south.

Agriculture is important, especially sheep farming. New Zealand also has large herds of dairy and beef cattle. Major crops include barley, fruits, potatoes, and wheat. But manufacturing is now the most valuable activity.

SCENERY
New Zealand's scenic beauty attracts many tourists.

North Cape

Whangerei

Gt. Barrier Island

Hauraki Gulf

Auckland

Hamilton

Bay of Plenty

Tauranga

East Cape

North Island

Waikato

Rotorua

RAUKUMARA RANGE

L. Taupo

New Plymouth

Gisborne

Poverty Bay

▲ *Taranaki (8,260 ft)*

▲ *Ruapehu (9,177 ft)*

Napier

Hawke Bay

Wanganui

Wanganui

Hastings

Palmerston North

Farewell Spit

Golden Bay

Tasman Bay

Motueka

Cook Strait

Karamea Bight

Nelson

□ Wellington

Blenheim

Westport

SHEEP
New Zealand ranks second only to Australia in the production of wool.

Greymouth

South Island

SOUTHERN ALPS

Pegasus Bay

Rakaia

Christchurch

Mt. Cook ▲ (12,349 ft)

Canterbury Plains

Canterbury Bight

Timaru

Milford Sound

Waitaki

L. Wakatipu

Oamaru

```
0      50    100 miles
0    50   100 km
```

L. Te Anau

Clutha

Dunedin

C. Providence

Invercargill

Foveaux Strait

Stewart Island

VOLCANOES
Taranaki (or Mount Egmont) is a volcano on North Island.

MILFORD SOUND
The coast of Southwestern South Island contains deep sea inlets, carved out by glaciers.

GEYSERS
North Island has many hot springs and geysers, which shoot huge columns of hot water into the air.

FACT FILE

● The Dutch, who were the first Europeans to sight New Zealand, called the islands Nieuw Zeeland after a province in the Netherlands.

● New Zealand's highest peak is Mount Cook, on South Island, which reaches 12,349 ft (3,762 m) above sea level.

● Maoris are a Polynesian people.

● No place in New Zealand is farther than 80 miles (130 km) from the sea.

● In 1893, New Zealand became the first country to give votes to women.

Arctic

The Arctic region around the North Pole includes the Arctic Ocean, much of which is covered by sea ice. Also included are Greenland, together with parts of northern North America, Asia and Europe.

Greenland is buried under a huge ice sheet. But the snow melts over most of the remaining land in the Arctic during the brief summer. Plants grow providing food for migrating animals, while the air is filled with insects, providing food for many nesting birds. The Arctic people, including the Inuit (Eskimos) and Sami (Lapps), once lived wandering lives. But today most of them live in permanent settlements.

FACT FILE
● The Arctic Ocean is the world's fourth largest ocean.
● The first explorer to reach the North Pole was US Navy Commander Robert E Peary on April 6, 1909.
● The sun never shines on much of the Arctic during winter. Between March and September, it shines on all of the Arctic for at least part of the day.
● The treeless region in the Arctic is called the tundra. Lichens, mosses, and small shrubs grow during the short summer.

POLAR BEARS *Large white polar bears live around the Arctic Ocean. They hunt seals and other animals.*

HUSKIES *Dog-drawn sleds were once widely used in the Arctic. Motor-driven snowmobiles are common today.*

IGLOOS
Ice houses were temporary shelters built by Inuit people.

KAYAKS
The Inuit once made boats called kayaks by stretching skins over a wooden frame.

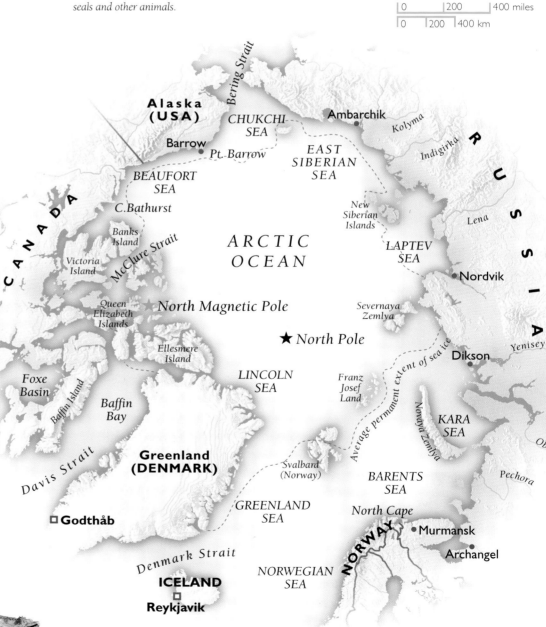

0   200   400 miles
0   200   400 km

Alaska (USA)
CHUKCHI SEA
Barrow
Pt. Barrow
BEAUFORT SEA
C.Bathurst
Banks Island
McClure Strait
Victoria Island
CANADA
Queen Elizabeth Islands
Ellesmere Island
Foxe Basin
Baffin Island
Baffin Bay
LINCOLN SEA
Davis Strait
Greenland (DENMARK)
Godthåb
Denmark Strait
ICELAND
Reykjavik
NORWEGIAN SEA
GREENLAND SEA
Svalbard (Norway)
Franz Josef Land
North Pole
North Magnetic Pole
ARCTIC OCEAN
EAST SIBERIAN SEA
New Siberian Islands
LAPTEV SEA
Bering Strait
Ambarchik
Kolyma
Indigirka
Lena
Nordvik
RUSSIA
Severnaya Zemlya
Dikson
Yenisey
Novaya Zemlya
KARA SEA
Ob
Average permanent extent of sea ice
BARENTS SEA
Pechora
North Cape
Murmansk
Archangel
NORWAY

Antarctica

Antarctica is the sixth largest continent and by far the coldest. Ice and snow cover 98 percent of the land. In places around the coast, the ice juts out over the sea to form ice shelves. Icebergs form when chunks of ice break away.

The icy continent has no permanent population, though some scientists work there for short periods. Only a few insects and other tiny creatures spend all their time in Antarctica. The continent's best known animals are penguins, which feed in the sea. Several countries claim parts of Antarctica. But none of the claims is recognized internationally.

PENGUINS

Four species of penguins breed in Antarctica. Others breed on islands to the north.

ELEPHANT SEAL

The southern elephant seal lives in waters near Antarctica. It is the largest of the seals.

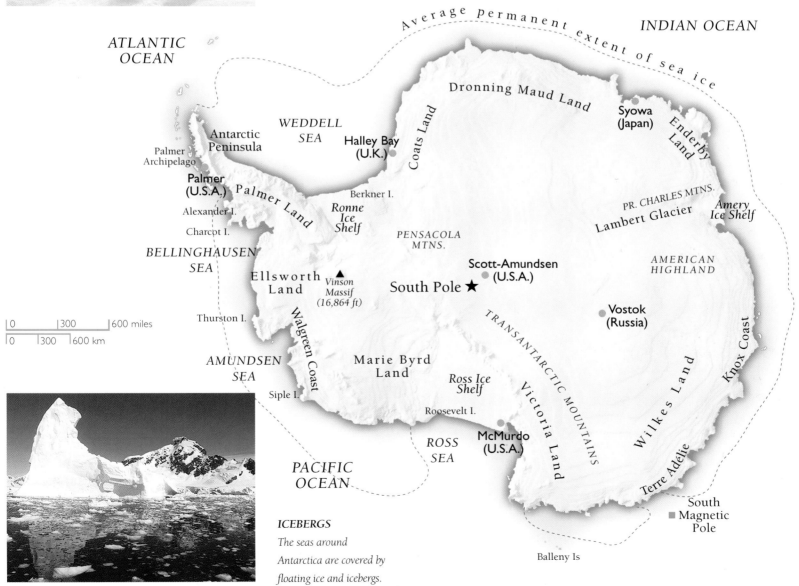

Average permanent extent of sea ice

INDIAN OCEAN

ATLANTIC OCEAN

Dronning Maud Land

WEDDELL SEA

Coats Land

Syowa (Japan)

Enderby Land

Antarctic Peninsula

Palmer Archipelago

Halley Bay (U.K.)

Palmer (U.S.A.)

Palmer Land

Berkner I.

Alexander I.

Ronne Ice Shelf

PR. CHARLES MTNS.

Amery Ice Shelf

Charcot I.

Lambert Glacier

BELLINGHAUSEN SEA

PENSACOLA MTNS.

AMERICAN HIGHLAND

Ellsworth Land

Vinson Massif (16,864 ft)

Scott-Amundsen (U.S.A.)

South Pole ★

0   300   600 miles
0   300   600 km

Thurston I.

Vostok (Russia)

Knox Coast

AMUNDSEN SEA

Walgreen Coast

TRANSANTARCTIC MOUNTAINS

Wilkes Land

Marie Byrd Land

Ross Ice Shelf

Victoria Land

Siple I.

Roosevelt I.

Terre Adélie

ROSS SEA

McMurdo (U.S.A.)

PACIFIC OCEAN

South Magnetic Pole

Balleny Is

ICEBERGS

The seas around Antarctica are covered by floating ice and icebergs.

Index

Pictures supplied by:
Peter Hince
Photodisc